Letting Go

Letting Go

Copyright © 2016 Joyce Wagster & Bonnie Jennings. All rights reserved.

No rights claimed for public domain material, all rights reserved. No parts of this publication may be reproduced, stored in any retrieval system, or transmitted in any form or by any means, electronic, mechanical, recording, or otherwise, without the prior written permission of the author. Violations may be subject to civil or criminal penalties.

Unless otherwise marked, all Scripture quotations are from the King James Version of the Holy Bible. Public domain.

Library of Congress Control Number: 2016941826

ISBN: 978-1-63308-235-9 (paperback)
     978-1-63308-236-6 (ebook)

Interior and Cover Design by R'tor John D. Maghuyop

CHALFANT ECKERT
PUBLISHING

1028 S Bishop Avenue, Dept. 178
Rolla, MO 65401

Printed in United States of America

JOYCE WAGSTER & BONNIE JENNINGS

Letting Go

*What Our Mother's Passing Taught Us
About Life, Death, Grief & Faith*

CHALFANT ECKERT
PUBLISHING

INTRODUCTION BY FORMER MISS SOUTH CAROLINA

This book has been forged through the unwavering devotion of two daughters to their mother's legacy, but more importantly to her life example. Aptly entitled *Letting Go*, it will inspire you as a reader to reach for the same principles that guided "Maw Glenn's" humble and less-than-idyllic life.

Maw Glenn seemed to be able to banish all thoughts of lack and found ways to inspire HOPE, CONFIDENCE, and ABUNDANCE into her own life as well as the many lives she touched.

I met "The Glenn Girls" when I was invited to entertain with their talent troupe that Maw Glenn organized. We entertained weekly at varying venues including nursing homes, jails, veterans hospitals, churches, prisons, hospitals for the sick and mentally ill and orphanages. We had fun and, through it all, we fostered lifetime friendships, memories, and life lessons of generosity.

For me, her most poignant legacy is that she taught me through her example the same theme found in the 13th century Prayer of Saint Francis of Assisi, "For it is in the giving that we receive." In the process of giving of my time and talents performing to those less fortunate, I gained invaluable experience and the confidence I would need to fulfill my dream of becoming Miss South Carolina.

I vividly remember when competing for the title of Miss South Carolina, the judges asking me what made me think I was best suited for the honor of representing my home state. I told them I was prepared to handle any personal appearance immediately because I had already been volunteering at the aforementioned institutions and my routines and full repertoire were on tape. Her example elucidated my purpose and became a blueprint for how I began to handle my life.

I thank God for placing dear Maw Glenn on my path as a young impressionable woman, and that Joyce and Bonnie are carrying her mantle onward. This book is about transformation and the courage it takes to continue the loving relationships we think we've lost when our loved ones pass on to eternity.

This remarkable book will be a gift to anyone experiencing loss and the grieving process.

Cyndi Anthony Bernard
Miss South Carolina 1975

TABLE OF CONTENTS

Dedication 9
Acknowledgements 11
Foreword 15
Prologue 17

Part I
WALKING

Chapter 1:   Musings of Early Years 23
Chapter 2:   In the Shadow of Dreams 35
Chapter 3:   A Journey Comes to an End 47

Part II
RUNNING

Chapter 4:   A Servant's Heart 57
Chapter 5:   The Spirit of Faith 89

Part III
REACHING

Chapter 6:   Blessings through Miracles 103
Chapter 7:   The Silver Cord is Loosed 121
Chapter 8:   Becoming Silent 143
Chapter 9:   The Gift 159

Part IV
FROM GRIEF TO HEALING

Chapter 10: Entering the Valley of Grief 171
Chapter 11: Facing the Firsts 185
Chapter 12: The Passage to Peace 193
Chapter 13: Reflections 203
Chapter 14: Signs of Wonder 211
Chapter 15: Lasting Wishes and Messages 223
About the Authors 231

DEDICATION

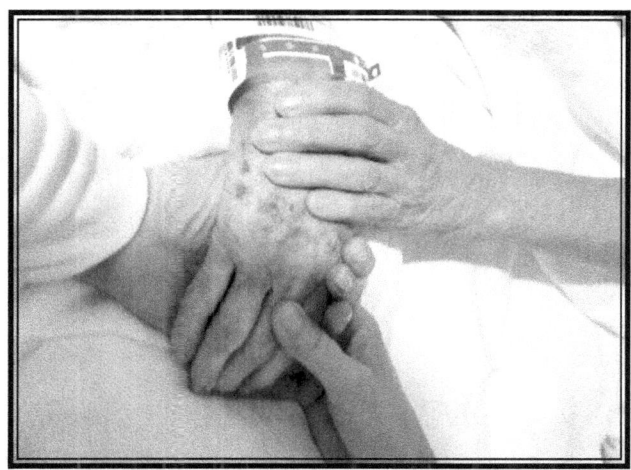

Dedicated to the memory of our beloved mother and to God, our heavenly Father, who reigns over the entire universe. We are forever grateful for the beautiful gift He gave us to share. No words could have expressed to us what her soul did—her passing was truly an event of heavenly measures by the divine hand of Providence: a miracle. We know now, in a way we could not have known before ... The soul is real.

And to you, the reader: Love your family and reconcile if you need to. The hands of God gave you to your parents, whose hands first held yours. Theirs are the very hands you may hold as they leave this earthly place to take the hand of Jesus, the Giver of eternal life. After all, that is what it is truly all about: moving to our eternal home.

So we are always of good courage. We know that while we are at home in the body we are away from the Lord, for we walk by faith, not by sight. Yes, we are of good courage, and we would rather be away from the body and at home with the Lord.
2 Corinthians 5:6–8, ESV

ACKNOWLEDGEMENTS

This book could not be possible without those who helped breathe life into it. We are forever grateful to Dr. Kitty Bickford for believing in our book and to our team at Chalfant Eckert Publishing for taking this rosebud and growing it into a rose. A special thanks to our graphic designer, R'tor John Maghuyop, for creating our elegant book cover and layout.

To those who helped walk us through the early process, we could never thank you enough for all your help: Pam McKoy, Brittany Gordon, Debbie Gordon, Linda Wagster, Lockwood Glenn, and Amy Ross Cook.

To our husbands, Tony and Larry, who endured our grief, our challenges, our discouragement and our sensitivities on this journey: your patience and endurance are forever appreciated.

To Mama's rainbows and sunshine, her grandchildren and great-grandchildren, Jason, Rebecca, Brittany, Brandon, Hannah, Bradley, Megan, Hayden, and Taylor: you were in our hearts each step of the way as we wrote this book about your "Maw Maw" who loved you so very much. She was very special, and each of you carries that special quality within yourselves.

To family and friends who had to hear thousands of times, "We are working on the book." Thank you for putting up with us these past two and a half years as we struggled with our growing pairs in bringing the manuscript forward. And we are so grateful to Dianne and Ray McKay who opened their home to us as a getaway to work through yet another edit.

Thank you most sincerely from the bottom of our hearts to all that touched the lives of our mother, whose names are too numerous to list, but please know she loved each and every one of you so very much and you were a sparkle in her life every day.

To Mary Barrow, Wanda Allen, Regina Cohen, Diane Rainey, AMVETS Ladies Auxiliary Post 2, Ernest Chavis, Cairson Brogdon, Martha Branham, Sharon Williams, Glenda Browder, Moise Perry, Janie Jeffcoat: What can we say…there are no words!

To Tiffany Lynch Ballington and Cheryl Applewhite Huizinga: Thank you for visiting our mother in the hospital and giving us another memory-filled photo.

To the restaurants which allowed us to spend hours with our computers and notes to work on the book, we thank you - Zesto on Forest Drive and Triangle City, and Tokyo Grill on Forest Drive and Dreher Road. To the Clarion Inn, Airport where we had to escape a few times to be still and be in the quiet to read, write and edit, thank you.

Thank you to Surfside Beach Hotel, where it all started, and to the Paradise Hotel and Sandcastle Hotel in Myrtle Beach, where we found ourselves listening to the ocean waves and watching the beautiful sunrises and sunsets as we continued to work on the manuscript. Everyone was always so good to us, even giving us a suite one time so we would have more room!

We would also like to thank these others for their specific and necessary contributions to our efforts:

Rachel Starr Thomson, Editor, Ontario, Canada

Laurie Horton, Editor, Tallahassee, Florida

Kimberly Cockerham — Foreword

Cyndi Anthony Bernard

Adam Lean - Marketing

Brad Wagster — Photographer

Megan Delaney - Photographer

Capsure Studios - Website Design - Larry Jennings and Keith Jennings

Angie Tindal - Graphic art

Copy Pickup - Marion Stoudemire, Owner

FOREWORD

I first met Ms. Glenn when I was an 18-year-old college freshman. I haphazardly entered her Miss Columbia Pageant, a preliminary to Miss South Carolina, because I was at home on Spring Break from college. I also entered because my mom, a pageant enthusiast, insisted and so … there I was.

I remember entering the auditorium and seeing this tiny, busy woman with a quick smile and even quicker wit. She was so passionate about what she was doing and told us that being Miss Columbia was not only a stepping stone to Miss South Carolina but was also a way for us to serve our community. She explained that the winner would be volunteering at the VA Hospital. She talked about the sacrifices that those veterans made for us to have the freedoms we enjoy and that this was our small way of being able to give to those who had given so much and to honor those who had given their lives. She described the incredible events that she hosted there and told a few stories of some of those heroes she'd come to know over the years. I wanted in! It was after that first meeting with her that I was determined to win her pageant. She had such a way of drawing you in without you even knowing it. I wanted to be around this woman and learn from her.

After I won that pageant and went on to win Miss South Carolina and Miss America, I always knew that a significant part of my success was the countless hours I spent volunteering with Ms. Glenn. I watched her give of herself with such joy. No matter how large the task, it was never work for her. She made those veterans, and anyone she came in contact with, feel special and loved. If you were fortunate enough to be in her presence, she had a gift for helping you see your true talents and showing you how to use them. In the many years, I was blessed to know her; she inspired me always to think of what I could do for others. As a young woman, being witness to her heart of service was something that changed me forever. It made me always strive to give of myself in that way.

Despite her commitment to the veterans, her greatest joy in life was her family. I so enjoyed hearing her stories about her very active grandchildren and the busy lives of her children. It was so evident that she loved them all fiercely and that she took such pride in them. She also instilled in them her love of community, as many of her children followed in her footsteps of being servants of the community.

This book reflects on the life of an extraordinary woman that came from ordinary circumstances. She had so many trials in her life but always was able to somehow reflect on others rather than herself. She truly touched my life, and I'm witness to how she touched the lives of countless others.

Kimberly Cockerham
Miss America 1994

PROLOGUE

Our mother was an ordinary woman—and an extraordinary one. Oh, how Mama made this so much clearer to us during those last few days we spent keeping vigil by her hospital bedside. Mama's life experiences included the whirlwind of one man's love in a cycle of marriage, divorce and remarriage, driven by the ups and downs of domestic abuse as her husband struggled endlessly with alcohol and drug addiction. Ultimately, she lost the only man she ever loved as he died at the young age of forty-six. Through it all, she worked full-time, raised four children and began God's work as a tireless volunteer, bringing smiles and laughter to many veterans, children and the elderly. For this woman who never drove a car and never had a driver's license, God always provided a way for His work to be done.

Our mother's rapid decline was a shock to us. Just two weeks earlier she had been given clearance by her surgeon after having hip surgery. She had also been cleared by her in-home physical therapist and passed her final exam beautifully. She went to her hairdresser and out to eat lunch—all in the same day! It was a celebratory day. On that Thursday, never in a million years would we have thought we would be sitting beside her only two weeks later in a comfort care room, waiting for her to leave us.

Many would say we were naïve, and they would be right. We just never saw ourselves living our lives without Mama. She was as vital, clear-minded and active as someone many years younger. Mama was our every day. She was a part of everything we did. And God had given her miracle healings before. Mama always came home.

Looking back, we can see that in that final week, God began giving us little signals to prepare us for the inevitable, but even then we continued to hold out hope. And then we found ourselves sitting by her bedside waiting for her to take her final breath. It was so surreal!

Mama was about to leave us! Oh, how we longed for a little more time! How could we let go of Mama? How could Mama let go of us?

This book is about our mother's journey and why every journey matters. She was a woman much loved and a woman of courage and strength, whose pathway through life was sometimes laborious and at other times full of joy, but was always inspiring. Through all the adversity she met on a daily basis, Mama was able to focus on doing good deeds. She was a volunteer at heart, a true servant. She loved her children, grandchildren, and great-grandchildren unconditionally. She loved the veterans and the elderly. She treasured her friends and, goodness, she loved the AMVETS organization! And she loved her one and only husband.

As we've written about the seasons of her life, we realize more than ever that God can use anyone He chooses and He will make a way no matter the circumstances. Mama's was not a life that was famous or that accomplished things you will see in the news, but one that did extraordinary works while being a simple ordinary person ... maybe not so much in the eyes of man, but certainly in the eyes of God. What is written in His Book of Life is what matters. Mama was a woman under the radar who fulfilled God's mission for her life and whose servant heart continues to live in the hearts of the many she touched.

We are just three daughters and a son who loved our mother dearly. Her passing profoundly affected our lives. With her death, we came face to face with a grief we had never met before, and an unexpected new season of our lives emerged—with a new awakening of purpose of our own.

For two of us, part of our purpose became telling Mama's story—to ourselves and to others. These words were penned from our hearts, in our signature style, and with God's tugging. This is our story and the events written herein are in regard to our own personal journeys. We have faithfully rendered our story and events to the best of our recollection, and in doing so, it is told in a way that evokes the real emotions we experienced.

With Mama's passing, we were set on a journey back to our challenging roots with her and our father to understand more of the woman she was and who we were in her. As the veil began to lift, we quizzed existence: What truly is this thing called life, and what is our purpose in this life? Our journey took us to places we hadn't been in a long time, bringing new revelations, joy and tears, along with some things that were bitter to remember.

Our mother's home-going was extraordinary—even miraculous, a most unexpected gift in her final moments. We are no more special than anyone else, but in Mama's last few minutes of life, God gave us something to be treasured. It was a spiritual gift letting us know she would be all right and, in time, so would we.

For our mother, it was a perfect exit. For us, it was a gift to be shared. If you ever doubted that we go from life to life, our experience may give you a renewed perspective that the soul is real, and we leave this earthly existence and live on beyond this life.

Like Mama, our ultimate goal is to end this race and run into the arms of our Lord and Savior, Jesus Christ; to have Him say, "Well done, my good and faithful servant! Welcome home!"

Our hope, as you camp out in these pages, is that Mama's story brings you peace, laughter, cleansing tears, joy, inspiration, memories of your own special loved ones and, most importantly, a closer walk with Jesus. Mama would love that. Perhaps light a candle in memory of a loved one or listen to some beautiful soft music as you meet our mother. We hope you realize that no matter what may have come your way, your journey matters.

Thank you for coming along,

Joyce & Bonnie

PART I

Walking

To every thing there is a season, and a time to every purpose under heaven: A time to be born, and a time to die; a time to plant and a time to pluck up that which is planted;
Ecclesiastes 3:1-2 KJV

CHAPTER 1

Musings of Early Years

I will lift up mine eyes unto the hills, from whence cometh my help. My help cometh from the Lord, which made heaven and earth.
Psalm 121:1–2 KJV

"I want my children to know they were my reason for living…"
Excerpt from Mama's last wishes book to her children.

It's 3:00 p.m., Friday, May 3, 2013. Life goes on outside these hospital walls. But in Room 6009, the beating of our mother's beautiful heart is about to cease.

The radiant spring sun shone through the window, cascading beams of light throughout the room and creating a most peaceful atmosphere, as Mama drew closer to entering a light even more brilliant to meet Jesus face-to-face.

It had been an arduous two weeks. Fatigued and weary, we had stayed the course. Our brother Lockwood had returned home brokenhearted. Deep down he felt the need to spend time with Mama's precious dog, Little Moe, fulfilling his promise to always take care of him.

As we looked upon our mother, it seemed so unfair to allow her to continue in this state of limbo any longer with organs failing and constant terminal congestion. Friday morning with heavy broken hearts, we discussed disabling Mama's pacemaker with her doctor so she could pass naturally.

When Mama's pacemaker was disabled, we were shocked when her body reacted as though she had been revived with heart paddles rather than moving into a deeper restful state. At first, we regretted the decision. She had been slumbering in a beautiful place of peacefulness, and the jolt had disturbed and startled her. But this would prove to be a blessed decision which opened a spiritual door to a gift from God through our mother that we will forever remember and share.

It is said, our eyes are the windows to our soul. Our mama opened her eyes for the first time in three days and began looking around. Her eyes were like glass and almost twinkling with a radiant pale blue hue with a brilliant aura. Mama should have been blind, yet she seemed to have vision as she looked at each one of us and about the room. Unable to move her head, she used only her eyes to look around.

"Hey Mama," Joyce said, sitting to Mama's right and holding her hand.

"We love you, Mama," Bonnie said from the foot of her bed where she held her vigil.

"Love you, Mama," Debbie cried as she caressed Mama's left shoulder.

"We love you, and we will miss you," we all said in unison as tears flowed.

All this interaction was bringing her too far back into our world, so we decided to speak very calmly and softly to her. Heartbroken, we agreed that we shouldn't talk to her much at all, as she needed to continue her transition in peace. It was all so mind-numbingly surreal.

As the room became quiet, she once again grew relaxed, and within moments she closed her eyes and fell back into a transitioning slumber. The room filled with a sense of serenity. There was only the soft whirring sound of the air conditioner as we each kept our place of vigil around our mama.

Grown daughters, we suddenly felt like young children again, remembering how she had been at our sides throughout our lives. Now we were at hers as she finished her journey here. As our time ran short, we looked upon this woman of great strength and faith in God, about to take her last breath, and tears flowed down our cheeks. Our eyes met, and our minds became as one. We knew this was not only our mother but a gracious soul, a soul that was about to journey home to heaven.

This reality came upon us with powerful force. Mama was leaving us. God was calling her home. This was real. Without speaking, we seemed to form an invisible tether around her as we traveled back to our challenging beginnings and pondered what had made our mother the woman she was and our relationship with her so strong. Why was it so hard to let her go? She had had a long life; we knew that, but our hearts told a different story …

Surely fall was in the air on that August morning in 1925, the morning of the twenty-fifth, when God chose to send Margaret Elizabeth Davis into this world, the day He began her long life journey, the day He knew He would be there when her soul came home.

This beautiful baby girl was welcomed into the world by Jesse Robert and Mary Magdalene Davis at 5:30 a.m. Her name had more meaning than we suspect her parents ever imagined: *Margaret* means "saint," and *Elizabeth* "oath of God." She was the second daughter born to them, followed by two more daughters and a son. She was a chubby little one with a fresh, even-featured face, and the freshness of her features remained through life. We know from pictures of her growing up that she was always neat and pretty, with clear blue eyes and beautiful cheekbones.

Mama as a toddler in her first season of life.

Mama's home life was typical of families during that era. The children were expected to help with all daily chores. Money was tight, and they grew their own vegetables; we recall Mama talking about shucking corn and snapping beans. The one chore they disliked to the core was picking cotton till their fingers bled. Her mother was a stern, strict, no-nonsense woman, and her father the complete opposite.

In those early years, Mama's family didn't have all the conveniences we take for granted today. They shared an outhouse and heated their home with a potbelly stove and kindling. Mama and her siblings wore clothing made by their mother, as there wasn't a lot of money for store-bought clothes. For the most part, they knew their place in the home and didn't question it. Everyone worked together as a family unit. Their mother's mantra was, "Lazy will kill you, but hard work won't." Perhaps it was attitudes like that which made the women of that era so strong and committed to their values. They were from an era that believed *idle hands are the devil's workshop* (Proverbs 16:27).

That work ethic didn't end with our grandmother as it would follow Mama her entire life. Her hands were never idle. She was always a worker, always a producer. As a teen, she took her work ethic into her first job, with the telephone company, and for the first time she was able to buy store-bought clothes. Her younger sister, Helen, still remembers fondly how Mama would share the new clothes with her. Helen was voted "Best Dressed" in high school because of Mama's willingness to share. That Mama possessed the heart of both a giver and a servant was evident even in those early years.

Hardships aside, while Mama and her siblings didn't have a lot, they were blessed with what they needed and never knew they were poor. Most importantly, they had a stable home life and knew they were loved. One of her sisters, Irene, in later years would many times jokingly say, "We were just too dumb to know we were poor." But perhaps they were just too blessed in other ways to give it much thought.

Mama was a determined person from the beginning, albeit she had a few kinks to work out as a spirited young girl while developing her can-do work ethic. She hated washing dirty pots, so on many occasions when it was her week to wash the dishes, she would hide those dirty ol' pots, determined to keep from having to scrub them. We could hardly believe that story when we first heard it—it was so out of character from the Mama we knew. But just as in her adult life, she willingly accepted the consequences that came with her choice.

Remembering when we had to do our chores growing up, we would write the chores down on little strips of paper, and on several of those little strips of papers we wrote the word "rest." We then folded them and put them in a bowl and took turns picking our chores. The more "rest" you picked, the less work you had to do. I guess we had a little of Mama in us in our early years as well.

Mama and her older sister Irene had an unbecoming habit of not hanging up their clothes, so one day their mother began piling them in a chair where they would have to search through the pile to find what they wanted. This strategy worked to break that habit, as the clothes would become wrinkled in the pile and the sisters would have to iron them. So they eventually started hanging their clothes up properly. This was another trait so unlike the mama we knew—she was the queen of ironing clothes till nary a wrinkle could be found!

Mama worked from dawn till dusk most of her life even in those final years. She enjoyed being productive in some way every day!

As a family, the Davises were a churchgoing, Christian crew. They were among the founding members of Greenlawn Baptist Church and attended every Sunday morning and evening, and every Wednesday night.

Mama's love for singing and dancing began as a young girl as she made her way to the stage as a member of the drama club in high school, participating in plays and musicals. When she wasn't on the high school stage, she was always creating little productions with her siblings, engaging them in some kind of singing and dancing. According to them, this was sometimes annoying, but they always gave in because Mama loved it so. But there was one incident of Mama's love for dancing that was never forgotten. Back then, they used what was called a "wash pot" for washing clothes. It was a big pot with a fire lit under it to heat the water. Well, one day instead of stirring the pot to wash the clothes, Mama was going to town just a-dancing and a-twirling all around that pot with a washcloth in her hand when suddenly her dress skirted the flames underneath the pot and caught fire. Fortunately, Mama escaped this scary incident with only some minor burns—and a lifetime of teasing about the time she was a-blazing and a-dancing!

Ah, the Mickey Mouse Club! Back in those days, there was a theater-based Mickey Mouse Club of which Mama was a member. The Palmetto Theatre was the local home for all the members to gather. All those who eagerly desired to perform hit the stage to a welcoming audience every Saturday morning. The club had a theme song, a creed, and promoted community service. We feel sure this ignited an underlying influence for Mama's purpose and joy for volunteer work.

One Saturday, Mama talked her youngest sister, Joyce, into singing "Oh Johnny." When it was time to perform, Joyce was struck with stage fright and refused to sing.

But Mama, well, she would have none of that, so up on the stage they went. Joyce recalls she started out okay, but the longer she was on stage, the stronger her fear grew until it turned into shaking, and soon she was singing "Oh Johnny" so fast it turned to gibberish. Needless to say, Joyce's affection for the stage wasn't the same as Mama's, and she never did that again. We can just see them now fussing with each other as they left the stage.

As a strong athlete, Mama consistently proved her skills on her high school basketball and track team. She was a mighty spirited runner with powerfully strong legs. She had an uncle who loved to challenge her to a race around the block with his car. Mama, determined, full of life and a fierce competitor, always won the race.

Mama walking down Main Street. A powerful walker too!

When Mama was twenty-seven, her mother died unexpectedly of heart failure at the age of forty-eight. Exactly sixty years later on April 23, Mama casually said, "Today is April 23rd, my mother's birthday, and she died three days later on the 26th."

Ironically, three days later on April 26th, our own mother would be admitted to the hospital for what would turn out to be her personal finale. As eventually happens in every life that passes through this earth, the earthly curtain was about to close. A new stage was being set for the curtain to be raised to enter heaven. Mama would soon take her final bow here and turn to enter the beginnings of a new production that knows no end.

As our hearts reached back into the past, we could hear Mama as a child and feel her youthful spirit, so full of hopes and dreams as she danced around her house—a house we too would enjoy living in for a while many years later.

It's funny how the heart yearns for so much during these final moments: wanting to feel every bit of her life, to feel her presence from beginning to end; and yearning to hear her conversations with her mom and dad and siblings as a young girl, a teen and a young adult. To feel the era she grew up in, the era of the 1920s, '30s and '40s when, as a family and a nation, they endured the Great Depression and World War II. We longed to embrace her journey from beginning to end. The end, at least, we would experience with her.

When we lived in the house where Mama grew up, much was the same as it had been when she was a child. Thankfully, the outhouse had given way to a bathroom added to a back porch area! We have some fond memories of our daddy during this time. Mama worked at the VA Hospital, which was within walking distance. At our granddaddy's house, although quite crowded, the four of us kids loved it there. We can still smell the scent of that home and see the large pecan tree in the yard. We played around that tree and gathered pecans in season. We fondly remember Granddaddy Davis sitting in his favorite chair with his dogs surrounding him as we all gathered around the TV every Sunday night to watch *The Ed Sullivan Show*, one of Granddaddy Davis' favorite shows. We loved it too. We particularly loved just having a TV to watch, even though it was a small one!

Flashes of memories of that vintage kitchen with all of us sitting around the table eager to wash down with a glass of cold milk ... a bowl of pinto beans seasoned heavily with salt, pepper, and fatback bacon, and enjoyed with a side of warm cornbread filling our tummies ... a poor man's meal, but a feast for us, remains with us to this day! Mama's cooking skills and thriftiness served us well during very lean times in our childhood. A hamburger for us was a treat. Mama actually created the original "smashed burger." She could squeeze that hamburger meat so tight between her hands and make it so flat you could almost see through it. You see, she had to make that hamburger meat stretch a long way. And to this day, we love true southern style seasoned pinto beans and cornbread and hamburgers smashed flat. It's sort of a badge of honor, reminding us of surviving those lean times. On days when we were wishful for something more, Mama reminded us that while we didn't always have much, there were always others who had even less.

Grandmother Davis passed away before we ever had the chance to love her, but we sure loved our granddaddy. Living in that house with him made up some of the best times of our tumultuous childhood. A treat we enjoyed was Sunday's leftover cornbread crumbled into a glass of cold milk. Mama and her daddy always preferred buttermilk with theirs, but we just liked plain old milk with ours. We frolicked and played around that house just like Mama and her siblings did so many years earlier. Sadly, the time would come when we had to leave.

We also attended the church where Mama went as a child. Transportation was a luxury for us, but we were able to attend Greenlawn Baptist Church whenever we lived within walking distance, even if it was a mile or two. The Reverend Jennings would perform the marriage ceremony of our mother and father not once, but twice. He was a kind gentleman, a very stately man and soft-spoken. To this day we can see his face and hear his voice. He baptized Mama and Daddy and in later years baptized three of us as well: Lockwood, Debbie, and Bonnie. Joyce was baptized later in her life.

Other aspects of Mama's childhood added color and flair to ours. Her love of theater and entertainment impacted us all and served her well into her future when she became involved with volunteerism. All her youthful singing and dancing prepared her well for dancing around like a clown, dancing the hula, being a pilgrim and creating many productions at the local VA Hospital. Her volunteer work provided an escape for all of us during very trying times in our childhood as we shared her love of singing and dancing.

Sitting by Mama's bedside and reflecting on her life and ours, we knew she had envisioned a much different life with our father and for us than what unfolded. But Mama made her choices in life, and she willingly reaped the consequences of whatever she sowed. She always strove to do the right thing no matter the challenge. She took responsibility for her life and her choices, and she dealt with them the best she knew how. Never did she see her life as someone else's responsibility.

Her message would be to learn from your choices, good and not so good, so that your path will become easier and your wisdom greater, to remember that we all reap that which we sow, that no one is perfect, but we can choose to follow the One who is—Jesus!

Mama began a difficult race in her early adult years. In many ways, the challenges to come would slow her life to a laborious, painful walk, driven by her determination and faithfulness. The powerful legs of her youth did not have an easy road ahead. When her physical legs began to fail her in her later years, she rarely complained about the pain—she just kept going, kept walking. That endurance would see the difficult years of her early adult life to their close and ultimately would carry her over the finish line of life. But long before she could get there, her life would pass through the shadows of alcoholism and drug addiction in the man she loved.

CHAPTER  2

In the Shadow of Dreams

"Even though your dad got his life so mixed up, I still loved him very much. We had some happy times together, and those are the memories I kept. He came into my life when I was 17 years old. I waited for him during WWII. We were married 2 years after he came home. You might say he was 'the one' for me and I knew this. You are his children and I know deep down in his heart he loved all of you. (We really loved each other, always remember this.)"

Excerpt from Mama's last wishes book to her children.

At age seventeen, Mama met the man of her dreams at a local skating rink. His name was John L. Glenn. Mama, of course, loved to skate, but Daddy was just hanging out at a popular spot. A young, good-looking man with dark wavy hair and dreamy green eyes, their attraction was immediate, and their love story began. However, a war was brewing, and she would have to wait patiently for him as he served our country in WWII.

Mama as a teenager ... beautiful and spirited.

On Saturday, February 22, 1947, a small but elegant wedding was held in the living room of his parents' home. Everyone said they were a beautiful couple, and in the only photograph we have of that day, we can see that they certainly were. When we look at that picture now, we know they envisioned an entirely different future than what would be.

Wedding Day!

What were their thoughts that day? We are sure they were ready to create a beautiful life with a home filled with Christ, children, love, and laughter. But in the shadow of this beautiful love alignment, a world filled with pain, challenges, heartache and disappointment was waiting.

Their family began to grow with their first son, Lockwood, followed by three daughters, Debbie, Bonnie, and Joyce. The hidden dangers and effects of mental illness from war experiences slowly began to creep in. These unforeseen forces would cripple our family life and ultimately create an unstable environment for our family to thrive.

Mama and Daddy as newlyweds and so in love

After graduating high school, Daddy trained at the Palmetto School of Aeronautics as an aircraft engineer, received his license, and became an airplane engineer mechanic. His duties were overhauling aircraft engines and inspecting aircraft. As a young man, he was proficient in this career.

But the war was calling, and few young men in North America would escape that call. A train depot on Assembly Street in Columbia, South Carolina, is now a restaurant—but it served as the place where most of the servicemen left this area to serve our country in World War II. This was the place where all the hugs and kisses were given to family members who watched that train leave the station, wondering if they would see their loved ones again. Our father's only living sibling today, Margaret Ruth, whom he affectionately called "Reet," recalls that even though she was only five years old, the memory is still very vivid as they all watched him, at the age of nineteen, leave on that train. It was the first time she had ever seen her mother and father weep. She said it was a sad trip home.

The love of Mama's life

Daddy was working at Hawthorne Aviation when the unthinkable happened. The Japanese attacked and bombed

Pearl Harbor on December 7, 1941. He called the love of his life, our mother, and his family to say he had enlisted.

After his training, he received his Gunner's Wings from the Army Air Field Flexible Gunnery School at the Laredo Army Airfield in Laredo, Texas. He volunteered for the Air Corps in July of 1943 and was called to active duty the following November. As a corporal, he served in Italy with the 15th Air Force after receiving the Silver Wings of a flexible gunner in Laredo and completing advanced training in B-24 bombers in Nevada.

As a tail gunner in the U. S. Air Corps, he was stationed mostly in Italy. Pictures, letters, and other things have been lost over the years, but Margaret Ruth recalls that he sent her a beautiful rosary from Rome and, most recently, she decided she wanted us to have it. Mama told us that most of his letters had large holes cut from each sentence, as that was the way the government censored things in those times. Wartime security was tight, and no information about where people were stationed or what was going on could be bandied about.

Many years after our father passed away, we found a letter dated May 1969, from First Lady Mamie Eisenhower, responding to a condolence letter Daddy had sent her upon the death of her husband, President Dwight Eisenhower. She responded to Daddy with a note of gratitude that acknowledged all his accomplishments. We know from this letter that our father was regarded as a war hero. We recently noticed the address on the envelope: it was addressed to our father as a patient in a rehab facility in Lexington, Kentucky. Still a patriot at heart, he took time to acknowledge First Lady Mamie Eisenhower in her time of grief. This was in 1969 when Daddy made what Mama thought was a solid recovery.

> (Military Decoration NOTE:) M. D. E. ((Gettysburg, Pa.))
>
> Your name, GLENN, John Lockwood, S/Sgt., Air Corps, U. S. #34841334 is among many World War Two heroes in which my Husband, then Supreme Allied Commander of all Armed Forces in the European Theatre of operations: personally presented decorations and citations as to bravery and exceptional performance in the line of "Military Combat Duty".
>
> I note, that you were awarded the "Air Medal"* (three times). The Air Medal, which is most honorable and distinctive, is awarded only to those members of the United States Military personnel for exceptional bravery, heroism, and metitorious achievement while participating in "Combat Aerial Flights."
>
> I also note, that you were awarded five (5) Bronze Stars, and the Presidential Unit Citation.
>
> Our Nation is proud of you and yours.
>
> Very Sincerely Yours,
>
> MDE/jww   MAMIE DOWD EISENHOWER

    War can take a toll on its heroes. From what we understand, Daddy was just never the same after returning home. He would vaguely speak of the bombs they were dropping, killing not just the enemy combatants, but innocent women and children. While he chose silence for the most part, there were times he briefly recounted the fear they felt as they were always under fire on each mission. He also, on occasion, spoke of the flak from the bursting artillery shells that filled the air. We have tattered, faded and torn photos he had kept in which you could see the night sky almost lit up with flak. Another trauma for our father came when one plane of the two bringing his troop home crashed, killing all aboard, his best friend among them. Our father was devastated at the loss of all fellow Air Corpsman and his best friend after all they had just survived.

    Old newspaper clippings recently found, although faded and torn, seem to indicate his sorrow. In those days he would have been classified as suffering from shell shock or battle fatigue. Today it is known as Post Traumatic Stress Disorder (PTSD).

Our father was never able to get his feet firmly back on the ground after the war. He attended school for a while on the G.I. Bill, but did not complete his studies. In between odd jobs, he would explore other possibilities. Once he came home loaded down with the first tape recorders made for the consumer market with the intention of building a sales career, but painfully hit a brick wall. He tried working at his father's service station but was never happy there and would talk about what could be.

He landed an opportunity to sell freezers, which believe it or not, were a novelty at that time. It was a great program that included food. He finally found success! With this company, he received several awards of recognition, including top salesman. Things were looking up and going his way. But, this newfound success actually opened the door for another problem to rear its ugly head. Mama suspected and feared the pressure to stay on top would lead to problems involving alcohol. And she was right. Eventually, his alcoholism destroyed his promising career. He always had great aspirations, but something he could not control usually derailed his dreams of long-term success.

For the rest of his life, Daddy's employment was never steady. At one point, Mama tried to be the sole income provider while Daddy stayed home cleaning, cooking, and overseeing us, in hopes of insulating him from the temptations of the outside world. Sadly, this was not a solution either. Because of his illness and work history, we moved many times during our childhood, with money always being an issue.

Throughout their marriage, our parents separated many times due to his addictions and the violent behavior that manifested from the alcohol and drugs. This created a dysfunctional home life rife with confusion and constantly missed opportunities for the family life we all so truly desired with our father.

Our relationship with our father is a case of a journey never completed. Even today we feel the emptiness and longing for what could have been but never was, and what will never be for any of us. For those left behind it is a constant haunting dream. It's a missing link that was never clasped onto the family chain. Underneath all those layers of addiction stood the man Mama fell in love with and the father we longingly wished to embrace.

To this day we cannot configure the exact timeline of our moves and the many events of our childhoods. We do remember that even when Mama and Daddy separated, he was never completely out of our lives. He was always around, not living with us, but always close. And when not drinking or taking any drugs, he was a good father, but when in the throes of alcohol and drugs he became unrecognizable. Yet we loved him. We still remember the times when he dressed up as a character in Jimmy Dean's hit song, "Big Bad John." A slender man, Daddy would stuff a pillow up under his shirt to give him a larger physique to portray this character. He chased us around the house and outside while singing at the top of his lungs. He would catch us and then release us to be chased again. He was very funny and loved to joke around.

One day, pick a day … any day, Daddy's car wouldn't start. Back then, if whatever jalopy we happened to have started, it was a good day. At that time, we had another very old car, and Daddy asked Bonnie to push-start his. He told her, "Now we need to get up to at least 35 miles per hour."

Bonnie replied, "Okay, Daddy!"

She got in the other car and backed it up the street far enough to be able to get the car up to 35 miles per hour. The plan was working well, up until Daddy started wondering what was taking so long. When he looked in his rearview mirror, he could see Bonnie coming at him full steam ahead. Before he could stop her, she rammed the back of his old car. Surprisingly, nobody was hurt, and there was little damage to either one of the old cars. After the shock had worn off, we all had a good laugh.

Our brother, Lockwood, was notorious for practical jokes and trickery, as was our dad. One day Lockwood rigged up a booby trap, expecting Joyce to walk through the door. It was set to go BOOM like a firecracker. But instead of Joyce, Daddy was the first person who came through the door and BAM! The booby trap worked but, needless to say, at first Daddy was not happy, but then he began laughing. This became a funny moment that was shared. Seeing our father laugh was a memory to keep inside our hearts.

"Daddy, will you draw us a picture?" Sitting around our Daddy, he would slide a piece of paper toward us, and we penciled scribble marks on the paper. We watched giggling with excitement and amazement as he magically brought his art to life drawing fluffy, lovely swans on the lake, trees filled with leaves, and even the faces of presidents. It's sad, isn't it, that he never found a way to use his talent? Sketching wasn't his only talent. Oh, his fudge! He was known for his delicious, mouthwatering fudge. One of our sweetest memories!

Daddy possessed many talents and skills and an entrepreneurial spirit. He always desired, more than anything, to be successful and provide for us. How disappointing and frustrating it must have been for him not to be able to conquer the very things that were destroying his hopes and dreams!

Over time, there was less of the good and more of the bad. As children, we didn't understand some of the things we saw and experienced. Seeing our father fall to the floor with a rapid onset of DTs (delirium tremens or drug/alcohol withdrawal) was frightening and like a scene being played out in a movie, but for us, it was real life. Our love for our father was filled with pain, yet we had a deep-rooted longing to know this person we called Daddy. Unconditional love echoed among the devastating effects of drugs and alcohol. It is hauntingly heartbreaking that we never fully knew our father, and that he never really knew himself.

It's hard to give up on someone you love, and it's even harder to watch him destroy himself. Our mother became our refuge. We clung to this woman we saw work so desperately to help and stand by the one man she loved while holding onto four children. Looking back now, we see through the eyes of little children how we learned to cling to Mama when things were scary and sorrowful. She became our strength, our refuge, our earthly savior, bonding us together.

The humble beginnings of their happy marriage faded over time as our father's challenges with substance addictions found a home. How daunting it must have been to struggle with the damaging thoughts that played over and over in his mind. With her children in tow, Mama met each challenge head on to the best of her ability. Several times she boarded a bus with our father to Kentucky or to other rehab facilities for treatment in hopes of getting him through his maze of despair, but it was a battle he would not win. He desperately wanted to overcome, but it was not to be.

During these years, doctors prescribed barbiturates (yellow jackets) to help those suffering from shell shock and depression. While our father was a good dad when he was sober, unfortunately for us, he had violent outbursts when he was drinking or taking barbiturates or mixing both, and we never knew when one of these episodes would manifest. There were many sleepless nights and many nights of fear. In the 1950s and '60s, people relied on family to help, as these situations were considered private and personal. There were no women's shelters at that time. Mama's father tried to help as best he could, but our family situation as a whole was just full of complexities. It is still mind-boggling today to sort through it all, so we choose to hold to the good memories and deal the best we can with the bitter ones.

As stated earlier, even though Mama and Daddy separated many times, our dad was always present in our lives. Life was complicated. In an attempt to send a strong message to Daddy with great hope that he could straighten out his life, Mama divorced him on June 21, 1966, and was given custody of all four children. He did not take this well, and the pattern of him still being in our lives continued.

A monumental event took place on January 1, 1967. Daddy rededicated his life to Christ with baptism! He poured himself into rebuilding his life by once again entering the rehab facility in Kentucky. His life seemed to be turning around, and things were looking up! And so it happened on March 14, 1970, with The Reverend Jennings presiding, Mama and Daddy remarried. This was so fitting for, in the last words she left to us, Mama told us that Daddy was the only man she ever loved—he was always "the one" for her. That was just the way she looked at her life with him. Even during the time they were divorced, she still stood by him and was always there for him.

The final months of our father's life yielded tragic repercussions. Shortly after they remarried, Daddy went to work at a service station. Mama had serious concerns about the influence of that environment as, in those days, it was quite common to hang out with the guys and enjoy a beer. She expressed her concerns to his boss and made it clear that he could not have even one drink. Unfortunately, her concerns were not heeded, and the temptation became too great. Anyone who has experienced the power and seen the results of addiction will understand completely.

At the same time, our brother Lockwood was in combat in Vietnam. This situation was totally overwhelming for our father. He worried incessantly about our brother being in combat. Simultaneously, Lockwood was extremely concerned about our father. Recently we found a letter from Lockwood when he was in Vietnam, dated May 1970, pleading with Daddy to stay off the alcohol and pills. He even wrote about the possibility of moving the entire family to California for a fresh start. He thought that would be good for all of us, and there were more opportunities there for everyone. No doubt they shared a strong bond and were worried about each other.

When the inevitable happened, it started the chain of events that would ultimately lead our father to the last leg of his race on this earth and our first experience with grieving the loss of a parent.

CHAPTER

A Journey Comes to an End

It was a warm night in the spring of 1970. In the wee hours of the morning, something was brewing beyond the bedroom door. Joyce and Bonnie awakened to Daddy murmuring belligerently to Mama and their faces drained with signs of disappointment. Daddy had been doing so well, but now ... here we go again.

Suddenly, Mama entered the bedroom, locking the door behind her, and laid down beside Bonnie. "Stay quiet and calm," she said, hoping Daddy would settle down, but his rantings became louder and strangely frightening, like nothing we had ever before experienced. He was like a madman. The smell of fear filled the room. Mama had always stood strong and firm against Daddy, but tonight even she was fearful as we huddled together.

Outside the bedroom door, we heard the unmistakable cocking of a shotgun. "We're going to die this very night ... right here" was the unspoken fear going through our heads.

Daddy was in a really bad way. We actually thought he was going to kill us, and we didn't even have a phone to call for help.

Suddenly, Daddy kicked the bedroom door open and began attacking Mama. As her adrenalin kicked in, Bonnie impulsively jumped up, got directly in Daddy's face, cursed at him and screamed, "Leave Mama alone!" This stunned him, and he immediately backed off and left the room, yet still ranting.

Mama told us to climb out the window, and she followed Daddy down the hall, hoping to calm him down and take the gun from him. However, still feeling an adrenalin rush, Bonnie jumped up and followed Mama, closing the door behind her.

Mama was not making any headway with Daddy. She told Bonnie to go to the bathroom and find hairspray to spray in his eyes or "anything to use as a weapon," hoping we could escape alive.

Bonnie went into the bathroom and shut the door. Mama went to the kitchen and started boiling water under the pretense of brewing some coffee to help ease the tension. But the real reason for boiling water was a defensive measure to douse Daddy if necessary so that we could get out of the house.

Confused, Daddy began banging on the bathroom door cursing and yelling, thinking it was Mama.

Bonnie, afraid to open the door, yelled, "It's Bonnie, Daddy … It's NOT Mama!"

He walked away continuing his raging rant and making accusations and threats. We have never forgotten those sounds and the fear we felt that night. We had never seen Daddy this out of control. There had been many violent episodes before but this one was one of the worst!

Joyce, petrified in the bedroom, had not climbed out the window but gently opened the door poking her head out to see what was going on. And there he was. Daddy was standing straddle-legged in the hallway with the shotgun. He turned and saw her and commanded, "Do not come down this hall!"

Joyce, standing in the doorway, frozen in fear, saw Mama backing up towards the front door with Bonnie behind her and Mama screamed frantically, "Go out through the window!" Joyce, scared and trembling, climbed out the bedroom window, crawled through the shrubs and ran towards Mama and Bonnie.

We scrambled into the car and locked the doors. Not surprisingly, the car would not start. So here we sat, in the wee hours of the morning, stuck with no way to escape and Daddy now standing in the front yard railing around with the shotgun still threatening us.

At this point, we are all exhausted, so we prayed he would go back inside and hopefully just pass out, a thought that was much too familiar. Mama rolled the window down ever so slightly to try to talk some sense into him and by the Grace of God, and we mean ONLY by His Grace, he went back into the house.

About that time, we saw a neighbor's light come on. Joyce ran to their house and asked to use the phone to call the county detention center where Mama worked and ask them to send help.

Years later, Mama told Joyce that on that night, Daddy had told her, "If they go out of the window, I will shoot them in the back." It was the most horrific night of our lives. We have never forgotten that night. Reality…the dream of our family being together was shattered forever. The marriage

Mama so desired was over. The dream Daddy had for family was over. It was over ... it was all over.

We have come to a greater understanding of the disease of addiction and PTSD today. Our father was no different from many others in that finding sobriety and then returning to alcohol and drugs, escalates the intensity many times over. That is why the rage we saw that night was beyond anything we had seen before.

While our father rarely harmed us physically, the verbal and emotional trauma were significant. Help came in the wee hours of the morning, and it would be the last time Daddy ever lived with us. This could not happen again, and Mama knew there was nothing more she could do for him.

Oh, how we wished our daddy could be well. It was such a constant confusing state of being. We wanted the good daddy we saw from time to time. It is very hard to watch someone you love destroy himself like a slow suicide. It took an emotional toll on all of us. That summer proved to be extremely volatile, as Daddy kept coming to the house trying to see us. Sometimes he was in a good state of mind; other times he would be in bad shape, and we would have to deal with him. It was hard to reconcile our desire with our need to be free of him because what we all wanted was for everything to work out with him in our lives. We wanted to be a family like we had seen in small glimpses and flashes of time.

Maybe the time was coming to make sense of it all. As a life without Mama drew closer, our father, long gone but never forgotten, held our minds captive. The things long brushed aside, because we didn't understand them or because no one really wanted to talk about Daddy, needed to come out where we could see them, talk about them, and seek for understanding. Maybe in so many ways it was just too painful, sad, and tragic. In those days, our lifestyle was looked upon as shameful and with scorn. No one knew about the hidden wages of war that could destroy someone and, if they did, it was just swept under the rug.

As children, we certainly didn't understand. Our little minds had to deal with our father's long breakdown. So many questions and feelings held so deeply within each one of us centered on the man who gave us life, yet left a hole in our hearts. We wish he could have seen the hero in himself and his bravery for undertaking such a dangerous position as a tail gunner. In spite of everything, his journey mattered. He made a difference with his service to our country, fathered four children, and was loved more than he ever realized.

We wouldn't understand many things about our father's mental illness until years later. But, still today, many mysteries remain. We are grateful for the good memories we have, because, through all the chaos and volatility of our lives, we truly did love him. He was our father. We know that for many it is hard to reconcile how we could feel this way, but when you are in an abusive lifestyle, it becomes both confusing and complicated, and only those who experience it can understand.

Today, we are still learning and growing in our understanding of WWII and all it encompassed. We realize now that December 7, 1941, the day Pearl Harbor was bombed, reached forward into our lives before we were even born and the alteration had already begun. Growing up, we knew vaguely that Daddy was haunted by the innocent people that had died during this war and that he felt responsible for some of those deaths that occurred during his missions as a gunner. But, a young mind cannot fully comprehend these things. The witnessing of countless horrors as the planes of those brave fellow gunners and pilots all around him were going down, the constant threat of being shot down, the guilt—true or not—of responsibility for the deaths of women and children ... we could not have begun to understand the toll all of that would take.

Our father dealt with these things in his head all our lives. He faced his fears on every mission and did his job, and that is a great testament to him. But he was never able to truly put the war behind him.

Years later we would learn when he was in rehab that he found it too painful to relive and work through the very obstacles that hindered his ability to heal. The memories were just too disturbing for him to tackle outright. When he passed away, we felt a sense of relief; not for ourselves, but for him. He didn't have to struggle any longer. His torment was finally over. Daddy was set free.

We grieved his passing, but we felt a peace for him. He had fought a battle within that he just could not win. For the four of us today, our memories and perceptions of our childhoods are somewhat different. Perhaps events and memories are suppressed. It is very difficult to map it all out.

Ultimately, we found our strength in and through Mama. She was a huge part of our lives, our very being. Was she perfect? No. Mama was juggling so much when we were growing up. Trying to hold it all together sometimes creates a very problematic environment in which to thrive. We were poor. We moved more than ten times during our childhood, including living in a shed at one point. Life was unstable in so many ways.

Our journey with our father was perplexing and bittersweet. To Daddy's credit, he fought for sobriety and healing, and he was a true patriot and loved this country. He once confided to

Mama after they remarried that if he could not break free from his addictions, he just wanted out. He wanted the Lord to take him home. He did not want to harm us, and he loved us.

He would never overcome the battlefield in his mind, and on October 20, 1970, at 2:10 a.m., just a couple of hours after his forty-sixth birthday, the Lord took him home. He died from severe lobar pneumonia, just as his little sister, Zivian, had thirty-eight years earlier. We also learned that he had pancreatic cancer and would have only lived about three more months. We believe God spared him that additional suffering and for that, we are grateful.

We were told that while Daddy was semi-comatose in his last hours, he fought the war, reliving those twenty-four missions that he was never able to make his peace with. We wish he could have seen the heroism in his bravery as a positive.

Honour thy father and thy mother, as the Lord thy God hath commanded thee; that thy days may be prolonged, and that it may go well with thee.
Deuteronomy 5:16 KJV

Preparing for his service was not easy for any of us. Mama, feeling the grip of grief, insisted that our brother take Daddy's wedding band to the funeral home and put it on his finger, and she wanted his hands positioned a certain way. She was adamant about this, so our brother drove to the funeral home at two o'clock in the morning, rang the doorbell and enlisted the help of the person on call to fulfill Mama's requests. Mama had told herself when this happened that she would not cry but shed tears she did. No matter what the years had brought, the love in her heart for the handsome young man she met as a spirited young girl at that skating rink prevailed. And in those final hours with him, she fretted over details. One thing she struggled with was frustratingly trying to get Daddy's naturally wavy hair to lay the way he always liked it, but she failed. It was so surreal to see our daddy in a casket. We all dealt with many mixed emotions as we numbly walked through this uncharted territory. And so it was, with our hearts heavy with grief, we laid our father to rest.

As Mama grieved quietly, she continued to forge ahead to keep from going under. She expressed her reasoning for her life choices and love for our father with the messages she had prepared for us before she left this earth, forty-two years later.

Mama's married life had been a tumultuous path. But there was a great deal of life still ahead of her. In many ways, Mama's best years—her "running" years—were still ahead.

> *Not that I have already obtained this or am already perfect, but I press on to make it my own because Christ Jesus has made me his own. Brothers, I do not consider that I have made it my own. But one thing I do: forgetting what lies behind and straining forward to what lies ahead, I press on toward the goal for the prize of the upward call of God in Christ Jesus.*
> Philippians 3:12–14 ESV

PART 2

Running

A time to kill, and a time to heal; a time to break down, and a time to build up; a time to weep, and a time to laugh; a time to mourn, and a time to dance;
Ecclesiastes 3: 3-4 KJV

CHAPTER  4

A Servant's Heart

The halls of the ICU are heavy-laden with anxiety, yet filled with emblazoned determination to beat the odds. It's the temporary dwelling place of families who learn to deal with swinging up to the sky on highs and hovering close to the ground on lows. Gathered around our mother's hospital bed, we learned quickly that every precious moment on this ICU emotional swing could bring something great, small, confusing, or dire into our world. Here, even a small positive update can be enormously uplifting. You learn to tune out as much as possible the constant bells and whistles of the medical equipment, reminding you that something in the loved one's body is amiss, along with the hustling of the medical staff working feverishly with each life hanging in the balance. Each room holds not only a precious life, but a family gathered together hoping their loved one will find healing and stay here a little longer.

Early on in the ICU, Mama's room was filled with that determination to beat the odds. We were relieved she had been moved here, as it meant more attentive care. Our hopes of getting past this huge obstacle of infection were at an all-time high. But the reality of the severity of this disease that held Mama's body captive was soon revealed through one simple photo.

Mama needed oxygen. Not only to help her breathe but for the benefits that extra oxygen brings to a body fighting an aggressive infection. She was pretty out of it at this time, but she knew she did not want the oxygen nosepiece, and she would use her right arm and push it up on top of her nose.

Joyce finding some humor in this grabbed her cell phone camera. Mama looked cute with her nosepiece on top of her nose like glasses. "She will laugh at this later," Joyce said, raising the camera with a smile and snapping a photo.

Glancing at the picture she'd just taken, Joyce's face went from smiling to grim as the photo captured what was beyond our physical eyes to comprehend at this stage of the illness. The photo revealed not the cuteness of the oxygen nosepiece being worn as glasses but the reality of a very mean, severe illness that veiled Mama's entire face.

Our hearts were stunned by reality. Sadness quickly swung the ICU swing down close to the ground ... and stopped. Mama was no longer Mama in this photo. It did not even look like her. It was our first clear reality check that something evil had entered Mama's body, and it had a firm grip. In great despair, Joyce quickly deleted the photo, and a saddened silence shadowed the room like a mist.

Our beautiful mother, who had breathed life into the world with such passion, now needed oxygen to help her heal—but perhaps she was indeed insisting, in her own way, that we allow her to let go.

It was surreal. As if in her silence she was speaking to us through the photo, "My children, please listen to me. Listen to me! I know you will miss me, but please…let me go! I'm fine! It's time to let me go." We weren't ready, but perhaps she was. The woman who was so determined to attend a VA Hospital program back in 2001, even though she was experiencing a heart attack and should have been on her way to the emergency room, seemed determined now to prepare herself for the life beyond this one.

We now realized that a photo taken of Mama when she attended the Valentine's Day program at the VA Hospital in February 2013, could very well be the last photo of her attending one of these programs. This picture captured what was stated in a letter many years earlier by a patient who thanked Mama for a great program: "From the looks of the patients, for a short time they forgot their own problems and had fun in their hearts along with smiles on their faces." This time it was Mama who was in a wheelchair and gazing at the patients in an even more special way than usual, and it was the patients at that Valentine's Day program who now gave Mama, even for a short time, a chance to forget her pain and her problems and have fun in her heart and a smile on her face.

One photo took our hearts away and was quickly deleted, but another photo would become a memorialized treasure, an image that would live on in our hearts.

Sweetest picture ever looking out at those patients.

> *"Our minds are sometimes limited in the natural to what God can accomplish; the ordinary made extraordinary through a consistent walk with God; beauty from ashes; function from dysfunction; a butterfly from a caterpillar; marathon from baby steps; running from walking. A person's circumstances do not dictate to God. God dictates through the circumstances."*
> Pam McKoy

In the early 1960's, God drew back the curtains for Mama to enter the world of volunteerism. While employed at the local Veterans Administration Hospital, she was asked by Mrs. Elizabeth Poat, a Red Cross volunteer, if she knew anyone who could put together a variety show for the patients. Boy, did she ask the right person! God knocked, Mama answered, and He set the stage for a long run of fifty-one years of volunteer service.

Together with her three daughters and two of their friends, Mama produced and directed the amateur group that later became known as "The Dollies Five." Just imagine this scene. With our little record player and 45 and 33 rpm records, we sang along with the artists and choreographed our own dances. These performances became a monthly event and provided not only a great escape for us but a wonderful experience for the patients.

Oh, how Mama's service taught us the gravity of volunteerism. With excitement, we invited friends to join us and be a part of the programs. Living within walking distance of the VA Hospital made it easy for us to get there. We loved it! There we met these wonderful veterans who had sacrificed so much for us and our country, just like our own father had done. Several times, he was one of the patients to attend our shows, and he was so proud of us. We loved seeing smiles on their faces and brightening their days, and they sure loved the refreshments served to them. We don't think they ever knew how much they meant to us by accepting us and making us feel special. Their smiles and compliments were like sunshine. They were happy and grateful for every little thing.

The patients began to expect to see us every month, and when posters went up that The Dollies Five would be appearing, audience attendance grew so large that the hospital moved us from the recreation room to the auditorium stage. In our own way, we were little celebrities.

Over the years, outstanding performance awards were presented by the Red Cross to Mama and The Dollies Five. For us, it always felt like we were walking the red carpet. Although we never expected to be recognized in this way, it was greatly appreciated.

As we look back at some of the pictures and the outfits we wore, we have to laugh. There were no funds to purchase stage clothes, and hand-me-down outfits were donated. For costumes we were creative, using felt material and glue. But it was never about the outfits or awards. It was about community service. It was about the smiles and the thank yous from all the patients who were always so very appreciative. This outlet was a blessing of great comfort for us because, for those short moments of time, we could live in a different place. All the while, another life existed for us. And now, particularly, we are grateful for all that time we spent with our mother, watching her come to life every time there was an event.

As these programs flourished, they included more young people, and after our father had passed away, God knocked again, and our mother's eyes were open to a greater vision. She realized there was a real need for volunteer entertainment and looked for ways to take her entertaining and uplifting programs to nursing homes and other facilities throughout the city.

While the VA Hospital remained the hub of Mama's volunteer work, the doors were opened at Crafts-Farrow State Hospital, the Midlands Center, the Babcock Center, the State Hospital, the Shriner's Hospital, various nursing homes and alcoholic centers. Yes, even though Mama never had a driver's license and never drove a car, God always made a way for transportation.

In 1974, Mama received a phone call from a young lady named Cyndi Anthony. Cyndi, a vivacious, five-foot stick of dynamite explained to Mama that she was the reigning Miss Lexington and her goal was to win Miss South Carolina in July of 1975. She had been told that if anyone could give her exposure throughout the state to meet the people of South Carolina in preparation to compete, it was Mrs. Glenn. Thus, a journey began, and a lifelong friendship developed with Cyndi and her family as we traveled the state visiting and entertaining patients at the Babcock Center, Shriner's Hospital, the VA Hospital, nursing homes, and many other facilities that welcomed us. God placed Cyndi in our path, and we remain close friends today. Cyndi went on to become Miss South Carolina 1975 and a top ten finalist in the Miss America Pageant. Today she still gives much credit to our mother for her taking home the crown and introducing her to the world of volunteerism.

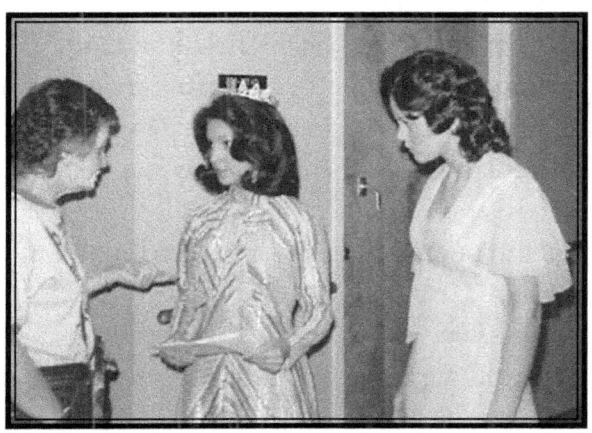

Mama as a clown giving Cyndi and Joyce instructions.

In 1977, Mama became a member of the AMVETS Ladies Auxiliary Post 2. After teaming up with the AMVETS, she coordinated bingo nights, cakewalks, birthday parties, carnivals, picnics and even Hawaiian luaus. She became a mastermind of activities and special ways to show veterans, underprivileged children and the elderly that they were loved and not forgotten. In the years to follow, she held the office of hospital chairman and served as the National Executive Committeewoman. She served as a Veterans Administration Volunteer Services Officer for the William Jennings Bryan Dorn VA Medical Center and also served as the local AMVETS Auxiliary Post 2 President for two years and as an Americanism officer. She also held the office of South Carolina AMVETS Department President for two years.

Those positions entailed many years of good works. Looking back, we stand amazed at all she accomplished.

Wonder what the Guinness Book of World Records shows as the most number of Ritz/Cheese Whiz crackers ever assembled? Oh goodness, how many cans of Cheese Whiz were used and how many Ritz crackers topped with Cheese Whiz were prepared over the years? How many goodie bags full of delicious treats were made? How many patients were wheeled to and from their rooms so they would not miss the shows? How many hugs were given to the veterans, nursing home patients, and children? How many Thanksgiving, Christmas, and special meals were served over the years? We don't know, but God does!

One of our sweetest memories was walking into Mama's dining room and seeing her completely surrounded by goody bags. If you could have seen her face, boy was she in her element, assembling over two hundred snack bags of potato chips, pencils, cookies, and anything she thought a child would enjoy. It was time for the Special Olympics, and one of the responsibilities and great pleasures of the AMVETS Post 2, was making each child a treat-filled bag of goodies. This had to be something very special as the glow from the dining room lights made the reflection of every little bag sparkle!

Her laughter can still be heard, as there was no place to sit as her goodies occupied every square inch of space. She had her system going, and we could not touch anything! We did, however, assist, guided by her rules. She did not want one child to be missing anything from their special bag. Her specifications and guidelines had to be strictly adhered to. We are sure that even today, her co-volunteers can attest to this.

We will never know how many kind words she shared during all those years. How much laughter did she bring to so many? How many people did she make feel special? To how many did she lend a listening ear? How many people did she show the love of Jesus through her simple gifts of giving? What a beautiful journey she had been on since 1962, the year God's call upon her volunteer life began.

A beautiful gem of a keepsake is a handwritten thank-you note from one of the patients who attended every program at the Veterans Hospital during his time there in the late '70s and '80s. It reads:

Dear Mrs. Glenn,

> I feel it appropriate to take the time out and say "thank you" for the fine entertainment and the warm, friendly feeling that was given to us in the rec hall through your leadership. It was thoroughly enjoyed, and about the biggest, friendliest party I've seen in some time. Your girls gave a fine performance, and from the looks of the patients, for a short time they forgot their own problems and had fun in their hearts along with smiles on their faces. I personally want to thank you for all the time you devoted to this and to the AMVETS who sponsored. You always do a fine job and even though you aren't told, it's always appreciated. I really enjoyed myself and will look forward to your return.
>
> *Charles*

Today we can still feel that auditorium filled with smiling patients, some who arrived depressed, some going through tough times, some without arms or legs and some even on stretchers. Yet here they came to take a break from everything, if only for an hour or so, to see a little talent show performed by amateur entertainers who were eager in their hearts to bring smiles and laughter to all the faces they saw in the audience as they sang and danced. To give these patients pause for just a short while, to serve them refreshments, thank them for their service, give them a hug, say a prayer with them, or even to help them eat or drink. How can anyone measure the worth of such a gift?

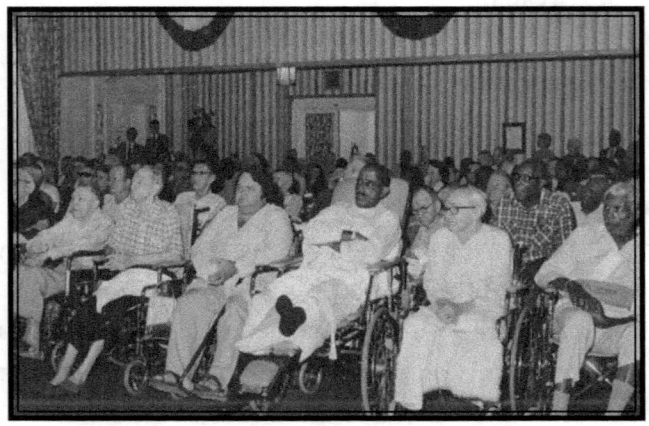

The patients filling the VA Auditorium once again!

We have the most precious picture of Mama in her Hawaiian grass skirt helping a patient drink from his cup. There are just no words to describe the beauty of volunteering and the unknown works that leave a lasting impression on a veteran, a sick child, or a senior in a nursing home.

If you give even a cup of cold water to one of the least of my followers, you will surely be rewarded.
Matthew 10:42 NLT

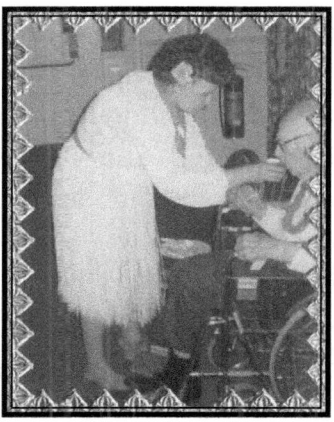

Mama helping a patient with his refreshments

And let the beauty of the LORD our God be upon us: and establish thou the work of our hands upon us, the work of our hands establish thou it.
Psalm 90:17 KJV

Volunteerism was a wonderful addition to Mama's life, and as she transitioned from some very difficult years into a new season, it took a bigger and bigger role. She and her co-AMVETS volunteers became lifetime friends and did wonderful volunteer work together. Over time they became like family.

People come and go in our lives, but some leave 'friend prints' embedded in our hearts forever. Such was the case when Mama met a vivacious lady, a fellow AMVET, Mary Barrow. They were two peas in a pod! Together they were a force to be reckoned with when it came to their volunteer service. These robust ladies were filled to the brim with a passion for serving.

Mama's final trip to the National AMVETS Convention was in August of 2012. It was held in Orlando, Florida. Ernest and Wanda, Mary's children, promised to take good care of her, and they sure did. She was so excited to visit the Holy Land Experience in Orlando and its productions, and she loved every second. Mama was like a vacuum pulling in all the life she could.

After Mama passed away, a dedication honoring her was held at the Veterans Hospital. Mary addressed that audience and shared some very interesting and funny stories, and she had plenty to share.

As a testimony of Mama's ability to make big plans and convince others to help make them happen, she recalled one volunteer program when Mama's planned presentation consisted of a mixture of a night of Waltz dancing and a Hawaiian luau! Mary jokingly said, "Margaret had asked her niece, Sandra, to come and dance the Waltz. She asked Sandra to wear a lovely evening gown and have her husband wear a tuxedo. Nobody else could have pulled it off!" Mary continued with a hearty laugh, "We all just did what Margaret asked us to do, but what I still can't figure out to this day, Sandra, is how you were invited to wear a beautiful flowing evening gown and I had to wear a plastic grass hula skirt."

A cotton ball for the WIN! When she was picking cotton as a young girl, we imagine our mother with her shoulder bag used to collect picked cotton and wearing a bonnet to protect her from the sun. She often shared the stories of picking cotton, remembering how the razor sharp bolls would cut into her fingers causing them to bleed. Oddly, cotton balls would play a big role in helping her friend Mary achieve a major life goal.

Mama was very instrumental in the steps that had to be taken for Mary Barrow to become the National President of the AMVETS Ladies Auxiliary. It would take five years to accomplish this goal. Mary's daughter, Wanda, recalls being at the National AMVETS Convention in Maryland that took Mary to the lead seat. Mama had called Wanda before leaving to go to Maryland and said, "Wanda, I need you to bring a billowing long gown like one you would see in the movie Gone with the Wind."

Wondering what in the world …Wanda did as she was told. Upon arriving in Maryland, Wanda, dressed in her Gone with the Wind gown, floated like a southern bell to the elevator and down to the convention ballroom. Once there, Mama placed a large floppy hat on her head and presented her with a basket of cotton balls.

"Ms. Margaret, what am I supposed to do with these cotton balls?" Wanda asked.

Mama replied "I need you to give each lady coming inside the ballroom a cotton ball and share the slogan for your mama's campaign, "This Southern Belle will serve you well."

So wearing the big dress, floppy hat, and holding a basket of cotton balls, Wanda became a Scarlett and did as she was instructed … not just one night, but every night of that week. The final night, Mary was voted in as the National President. Wanda said it was worth every cotton ball she handed out and every sharing of the slogan to every lady who came into the room.

From a young girl wearing a floppy hat picking cotton till her fingers bled to the soft balls of cotton combined with a sweet slogan, Mama's determination and leadership took her friend Mary to the winning seat. These two ladies, soft yet strong, intertwined with a friendship of give and take, shared a bond for over 35 years, reminiscent of something as simple as that of ... a cotton ball.

Wanda shared these words for us:

"I am so glad I was with Ms. Margaret at the last convention she was able to attend. I loved her so much, and it seems to me that I can hear her sometimes tell me when I am down, 'Don't worry about it Wanda Gail, it will be alright.' She could make me laugh no matter what, she would tell me some crazy funny story, and we would laugh and laugh. Today, when I am at the VA for the monthly Bingo program, I try to do everything as if Margaret was there. I can almost feel her around me when I am standing in the kitchen preparing the plates of food for the patients. Memories I hope I never forget. I so love your mother, thank you for sharing her with us."

In those final months of Mama's life, Mary and other AMVETS volunteers were like medicine to her. When Mary, Regina, Diane, Wanda, or one of her co-volunteers called, she perked up with a vibrant energy, allowing her to forget her pain for those few moments.

> Lo and behold ... Mama left no stone unturned when it came to creating and directing special programs and events. In this book, we can only list a sampling of the service our mother had such a passion for but we wanted to share some of the highlights with you!

Because We Care Day! Mama directed this local annual event founded by the National AMVETS Organization in which every patient in the hospital was visited and given a personal care kit. This all day event closed with live entertainment in the auditorium. It was repeated on the *Salute to the Hospitalized Veterans* on Valentine's Day.

King for a Day! Mama created the King for a Day Award, an event in which all wheelchair patients of the Nursing Home Care Unit of the VA Hospital were treated to a banquet, where each one was crowned and presented with a merit award certificate. A special program was presented in appreciation for their service to this country. When our granddaddy, our mother's father, became a patient in the Nursing Home Care Unit, she was able to create a fond memory of him as she crowned him King for a Day. A treasured photo of Granddaddy Davis in his wheelchair, wearing his crown, with Mama behind him and her hands lovingly on his shoulders is priceless. What a wonderful opportunity it was for her to recognize her veteran father during some very difficult times for him in his last days among us!

Veteran of the Month! Every single month a celebration was held honoring a veteran chosen from the Nursing Home Care Unit. The Veteran of the Month received special recognition for his or her service and was given an original poem penned by Mama reflecting their uniqueness and was presented with a plaque and gifts.

Mama presenting The Vet of the Month Award

The Escort Services Program! Hold on! Don't get the wrong impression. It's not what you think! On her assigned Sunday or when otherwise called upon, Mama made her way to the VA Hospital for the Escort Services Program, where she helped push wheelchair patients to the chapel for church services and then back to their rooms.

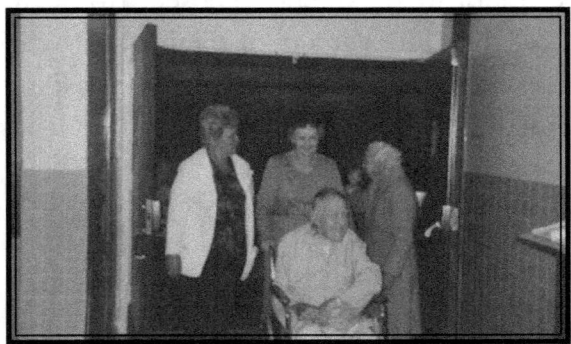

Pushing patients in wheelchairs on Escort Sundays so the patients could attend church!

These are cherished memories of years long gone now, with so many volunteers and patients having passed on, but they all left something special behind. For just one sparkling moment of love and laughter shared both ways surely must live on in the energy around us. Whatever would this life look like if it lacked this beautiful sprinkling of glitter - of the things given freely with value beyond measure?

Fundraising was an art Mama became well-versed in for raising the additional funds needed to carry out the AMVETS Post 2 volunteer activities. Pageants became a united force for fundraising and expanding community outreach. This expansion engaged the volitional hearts of many young people, some as young as three years of age. She was a great teacher of the sanctity of community service, patriotism, and love of country. She had a deep appreciation for our veterans, the elderly, and the mentally and physically challenged.

For well over twenty years, Mama produced and directed charitable pageants. The winners would make appearances at all the volunteer programs and tour the VA Hospital and nursing homes, where they would give the patients little gifts and enjoy conversation with them. Among the pageant titles were South Carolina Clover Princess, South Carolina Angel of Beauty and South Carolina Angel of the Universe.

It was a night of glamour, or so we thought. Mama and her sidekick, Kaye Mason, look regal in our post-pageant ritual - eating at Ryan's Steakhouse. As Mama and Kaye navigated the salad bar, they strutted proudly in their blue and black glittery tops that Kaye had made special for them to wear that day. Heads turned, whispers were heard. Suddenly, Joyce caught a glimpse of what looked like a serious situation here! There was a lot of exposure going on! When everyone was once again seated at the table, Joyce did further investigation of the exposing, and she noticed the fabric of Mama's and Kaye's tops had somehow disintegrated under their arms and down their sides with only little pieces of threading holding them together, putting a lot of skin and bras on display. "Oh my goodness," Joyce thought. Then she leaned and whispered almost laughing, "Mom, what in the world is going on with y'alls' tops?"

Mama lifted her arm and exclaimed, "Oh my word, Kaye, look under your arms."

Their faces exploded with laughter as did our entire table. Let's just say exhaustion can make a "spit-food-out-of-your-mouth" moment even more hysterical. As we say in the South, "Bless their hearts!" They had been so proud of their glittery blue and black tops Kaye had designed and made special for them to wear that day!

There she is ... for fifteen years the AMVETS Post 2 held the franchise to the Miss South Congaree and Miss Columbia preliminary pageants to the Miss South Carolina Pageant, affiliated with the Miss America Scholarship Organization. Mama was the pageant producer and director. She, along with the wonderful team of AMVETS Post 2, crowned many beautiful young ladies. They loved and supported all their contestants and titleholders.

In 1993, a lovely young lady, Kimberly Aiken, competed in the Miss Columbia Pageant. This dynamic eighteen-year-old would go on to capture the title of Miss South Carolina and Miss America 1994! It had been twenty-seven years since Miss South Carolina had won the coveted Miss America title (the last one was Marian McKnight in 1957). What a thunderous celebratory evening was had by all who attended and by those sitting in front of their TV sets at home. Oh, what a sweet legacy for Mama, Mary, and the AMVETS Auxiliary Post 2. There has not been another Miss South Carolina to bring home the Miss America crown since Kimberly Aiken, but some have come close.

Kimberly Aiken Cockerham. From Miss Columbia to Miss South Carolina all the way to winning the Miss America title in 1994! Still exciting to this day!

Little Miss Volunteer! Oh, how Mama meticulously kept records of every appearance made. And at the end of the year, she presented her junior volunteers with civic awards in appreciation of their time and talents. Whoever made the most appearances received the recognition of Little Miss Volunteer receiving a trophy, a pearl crown adorned with the AMVETS emblem and the honor of making appearances for the next year with this prestigious title.

Patriotism! In 1980, Mama donated our father's American flag to fly in the Avenue of Flags at the VA Hospital. She always took part in Love America Week at a local elementary school by presenting a flag to the school and plaques and lapel pins to every student.

Mama's patriotism abounded as she coordinated the Americanism Awards, in which students were invited to write essays on "What America Means to Me" or "What Being a Volunteer Means to Me." These essays were judged, and the winners were presented their awards at a banquet. Through these youth programs, Mama hoped to bring more and more young people into the hearts of others and to involve the hearts of others with more and more youth. Even today, many former volunteers speak of how wonderful the experience was and how much they still love Mrs. Glenn. Tracey Marie Luther (Mack), who was eleven years old at the time, won the Joyce S. Goodwin Volunteer Award, AMVETS Auxiliary, 1983–1984, for her essay on "What Being a Volunteer Has Meant to Me."

WHAT BEING A VOLUNTEER HAS MEANT TO ME!

I would like to say that my work with the AMVETS has played an important role in my life. It has taught me how to share my love with other people regardless of whether or not I know them. I appreciate Mrs. Glenn and all the AMVETS for all the hard work they put into caring for other people.

Being a volunteer has meant spreading love and joy to those who took time from their lives to defend our country and help keep America free. It has meant sharing kindness and laughter with those who are sick and sometimes very sad. Being a volunteer has meant having fun and making many wonderful friends. Being a volunteer has meant caring.

One special thing being a volunteer has meant to me is having the love of Mrs. Glenn and all the AMVETS ladies. Knowing that what I do helps them in their volunteer work has meant a lot to me.

My volunteer work is very important to me and has been an important part of my life since I was very small. My entire family has become involved in my volunteer work, and this makes it very special.

To close, I want to say that although this paper has been worded "has meant" all the way through, my volunteer work *means* more to me than I can fully express in words. I plan to continue my volunteer work as long as Mrs. Glenn and the AMVETS will have me. Being with my friends and spreading our love for each other out to the patients we entertain makes me feel great. Being a volunteer has meant getting "high" on love and spreading that feeling wherever I go.

Tracey Marie Luther
AMVETS Youth Volunteer

Volunteering can leave lasting impressions, and some of these grow into new and lasting works. Lindley Mayer was another whom Mama introduced to volunteerism at the early age of three. Lindley has continued her volunteer work and created her own charity, L.A.D.Y. Bugs Across America, Lindley's Alliance for Disabled Youth, helping children with disabilities. She has two siblings with disabilities and understands their challenges firsthand. Lindley won the title of Miss South Carolina United States in 2016 and was awarded the Presidential Lifetime Achievement Award having logged over four thousand hours of volunteer service.

Lindley's precious thank-you note, written in 1998 when she was just eight years old, speaks to how those early years of volunteer workflow through her today.

Lindley's thank-you note in 1998 to Mama:

> TO: Mrs. Glenn
> You are the best Pajeant Director in the world! Thank you for always being so sweet to me. I am so happy to be able to be one of your ANGEL OF THE UNIVERSE Queens. It makes me fed so good inside my heart to help the sweet patients at the V.A. Hospital. They have the sweetest smiles. You have given me this opportunity. I hope I can be your queen again someday. You are the flower in my heart.
>
> I Love you Lindley Mayer 1998.

IN REMEMBRANCE OF
MAMA FROM LINDLEY ...

I have always been taught that it is not what we have in life but WHO we have in our lives that matters. Mrs. Glenn was one of the most nurturing, caring, and selfless women that I have ever known, and she made an incredible impact on who I am today. She introduced me to volunteering at the age of 4 by taking me with her to the Veteran's Hospital in Columbia, SC. We went from room to room visiting with the veterans and even at that young age I began to realize the importance of making other people smile. Mrs. Glenn brought so many smiles and laughs to every person that she met, and I wanted to follow in her footsteps. She gave of herself each and every day and had the biggest heart. She took time with me to teach and inspire me, and for that, I am forever grateful. It was because of her guidance that I founded my very own non-profit organization called Lindley's Alliance for Disabled Youth in honor of my two special needs siblings. She taught me the importance of raising funds, bringing hope and raising awareness for all people in need. Since 2005, when Lindley's Alliance was founded, we have been able to raise over $80,000, and I know that Mrs. Glenn would be so proud. I will continue to live out her legacy and teach others what she always taught me.

Lindley

It has been said a picture is worth a thousand words, and tens of thousands of these "words" speak volumes to the service Mama and the AMVETS Ladies Auxiliary Post 2 fulfilled. Scrapbooks Mama created, lined with years of photographs, bring all these good works to life.

Pages and pages full of memories of smiling patients and intriguing images of Mama and the AMVETS ladies dressed as clowns, hula dancers, pilgrims and other characters, smiling and laughing - brimming with the true spirit of giving.

Mama had eyes like a hawk, and when she noticed a patient who looked sad, she shimmied, hula danced, jitterbugged, or did whatever necessary to bring a smile forward.

If the patient was in a wheelchair, she took their hand and did a little jitterbug or shag with them. It wouldn't take long before a beautiful smile would emerge on the patient's face. You see, hospital stays could be long or permanent and lonely for some, and that's one reason these programs were so significant.

Besides involving children in volunteer work, Mama also made a great effort to impact children with special needs. At least once a year, she, along with Mary Barrow, threw the children at Miracle Hill a big party and surprised them with gifts, games, bags of treats, and lots of hugs and love.

Mama had a warm heart for the children in the Special Olympics and for three years in the 1980s, she co-directed the Special Olympics State Finals Dance, which hundreds attended.

The South Carolina State Fair! To brighten the day of 50 special needs children, Mama always looked forward to coordinating and attending the South Carolina State Fair with her daughter Debbie who was a special education teacher. Although Mama did not drive, she rounded up all the transportation and chaperones needed for a day at the Fair with Debbie's class and another class for handicapped children. They filled 50 tummies with cotton candy, candied apples, french fries, corn dogs, and topped it off with ice cream. You know, all the 'healthy' fair foods! If you could have seen their faces light up as they enjoyed the food and the sights and sounds coming from the rides and special shows, you would understand why Mama loved this occasion so!

Just a little ways down the road … yes, since Mama didn't drive, she always thought everywhere she had to go was 'just a little ways down the road.' Being from the south, we always enjoyed eating out after an event. An event … any event! It did not matter! One event in particular stands out. We all gathered at Shealy's Restaurant after attending her granddaughter Brittany's dance recital in Batesburg. After we had stuffed ourselves, Mama calmly and casually chimed in and asked her son-in-law Scott to take her 'just a little ways down the road.'

When he asked where she needed to go, she said Fort Jackson to the Special Olympics event. "Fort Jackson! That's forty-five miles away!"

She nodded and smiled and said, "Well, it's not that far!"

We all laughed, and Bonnie volunteered to take her. To Mama, the people at these events were most important, and we never regretted those trips that were 'just a little ways down the road.'

Mama certainly had a sweet way of asking people to help with what needed to be accomplished. She knew how to delegate, get things done, and lead in such a way that people eagerly wanted to follow her. Even when she needed entertainers, it didn't matter if they had to waltz, be a clown, hula dance, portray a 50's character, shimmy or shag, or even wear ridiculous outfits; they played along with joy in their hearts! Perhaps that determined young girl, who so many years earlier had such convincing ways, was now using her skills to serve her well in God's purpose for her life in this world of serving others. Her children and the AMVETS ladies were willing partners in bringing her themes to life. Mama was creative. Yes, very creative, as we recently found pictures of her and Mary at a National AMVETS Convention costume party seemingly dressed as "Playboy bunnies," although very decently! There are so many precious and hilarious memories that live on in these innocent photographs.

AMVETS AUXILIARY Post 2 ... Country Night

The crispness of autumn was in the air. Warm summer breezes shifted into a new fall season. Mama loved this time of year and the scent of fall candles, the color changing of leaves, and decorating with pumpkins and scarecrows! It was also time for the big Halloween program for the veterans at the VA hospital. In preparation, a trip to the Dollar Store was a must. Mama's usual side-kick, Regina Cohen, was not available on this day so Brittany, Mama's granddaughter, was happy to help her and spend time with her! When they arrived at the store, Brittany asked: "What do you want me to get, Maw Maw?"

Mama answered, "Honey, you can go find me some fall colored plates, orange and yellow but listen here...DO NOT get the cheap ones."

Brittany, with a puzzled look on her face, responded, "Uh, Maw Maw, maybe you don't realize it, but it's a dollar store, they are all a dollar!"

Mama responded with a chuckle, "Oh Brittany, you know what I mean. I want the plastic plates! You get more with the paper plates, but the plastic ones are better!"

Brittany laughed and gave her Maw Maw a tight hug! It was just one of those sweet moments like 'just a little ways down the road.'

And whatsoever ye do, do it heartily, as to the Lord, and not unto men: knowing that of the Lord ye shall receive the reward of the inheritance: for ye serve the Lord Christ.
Colossians 3:23–24 KJV

Mama's tireless work continued even after being stricken with rheumatoid arthritis. She was amazing at pushing through pain, striving to continue her loyalty to volunteer service and staying active and productive, which she surely did.

At the age of seventy-six, Mama had a heart attack and was told after the CATH that there was nothing they could do for her. But Mama beat the odds and received a miracle, and she persevered and continued her volunteer service. We believe this service gave breath to her life.

Many of the programs Mama initiated ended over the course of time. Things began to change even in the manner you could volunteer at the VA Hospital. So everyone adapted, and the monthly bingo and refreshment program continues to this day with the remaining AMVETS Post 2 volunteers at the helm.

There is something to be said for accomplishing things that many see as ordinary. We are not all called to be a David,

Abraham, Moses, Joseph or Deborah, yet that does not mean we are without importance. Always remember that even if you are one of the least of these, you can make a difference in this world. God needs vessels of all types. We look back on so many little things, so many little memories, yet they are enormous in scope when we look at the works that were accomplished in fifty-one years. Until retirement, during many of these years Mama worked a full-time job and sometimes two jobs.

Whatsoever thy hand finds to do, do it with thy might.
Ecclesiastes 9:10 KJV

Mama wrote in one of her scrapbooks on July 28, 1979: "'In the Good Ole Summertime' off we trotted again to try to make the patients happy. With us, we carried talented young ladies. We sang and danced and chatted with all the patients. Afterward, refreshments were served, and we sang and danced some more."

Mama herself was one of the least of these. There were many times when Mama set her own problems aside to put a program together. One would never know what she was dealing with because she didn't take it with her. She put the patients first, knowing she would come home to deal with what was going on in her own life. She never had much, she struggled financially throughout her life, and she certainly had her share of problems, but she somehow was always able to find joy in the Lord, her family, her friends and in her purpose and still deal with whatever it was she had to deal with.

She learned to live life through all kinds of circumstances, major obstacles and a lot of hardships. That's just the way

Mama rolled, and we rolled right along with her. Isn't that what we are called to do? Count it all joy even in trials. She certainly did that!

And God is able to make all grace abound toward you; that ye, always having all sufficiency in all things, may abound to every good work.
2 Corinthians 9:8 KJV

Mama's message would be to be a light for someone. To be an angel who brings good tidings to someone who needs it; not for accolades, but because it is a treasure you won't find anywhere else and because it brings glory to God.

A note left for us upon our Mother's passing says it beautifully:

"Ms. Margaret will be missed. Her patriotic tireless giving to the Veterans is truly a life we should all strive to emulate as a means of giving back to our nation's finest."
(Posted by Tammy Finney – Columbia, SC, May 6, 2013)

God led Mama into the beautiful and rewarding land of volunteerism in the early 1960s. He gleaned what to the world was a seemingly ordinary life and turned it into a rich harvest to touch the lives of many. He showed us what He could accomplish through one woman who chose to believe Him, to take her into other people's lives in a world that depended on automobiles and a driver's license when she had neither—an ordinary woman with such a passion for giving. He directed her to extraordinary works, not by the measures of the world but by heavenly measures. He showed her how to create something good out of our father's struggles and early death. She believed in God and kept putting one foot forward until she used those feet up to the end. Mama knew she wasn't perfect, but she chose to walk with the One who is, and now she is running with Him!

---

*And we know that all things work together
for good to them that love God, to them who
are the called according to his purpose.*
Romans 8:28 KJV

Mama is living proof that when a heart stops beating here, through the legacy left, it will continue beating through others because of the love extended to them. It's amazing how a life, even after passing away, can continue to touch the lives of so many. It's proof that every journey matters to somebody. We continue to this day to hear from people who knew Mama and who remember their days of volunteering through her enlistment as some of the best memories of their childhood. It would be impossible to cover all the works Mama accomplished in this one chapter, but our hope is to encourage others to find a place, in some big or small way, in this world of selfless giving.

Mama never stopped, but…she was stopped. In February 2013, Mama attended her last program at the Veterans Hospital, ending fifty-one years of volunteerism. Her season of giving had come to an end.

...Blessed are the dead which die in the Lord from henceforth: Yea, saith the spirit, that they may rest from their labours; and their works do follow them.
Revelation 14:13 KJV

Be ye strong therefore, and let not your hands be weak: for your work shall be rewarded.
11 Chronicles 15:7 KJV

CHAPTER 5

The Spirit of Faith

"You never know how strong your faith is until it has been challenged beyond anything you could have imagined."
Bonnie Jennings

The emergency room once again, only days after we thought Mama had made a miraculous recovery. Mama is so weak in the waiting room, and we know something has gone horribly wrong. Her neck and shoulder are frozen in pain, and she looks so tired and so disheartened to be here again. It is hard even to look at her face. Knowing deep within that this could be a very serious situation; we carefully display our bravest faces.

As that night progressed and Mama was admitted, her situation worsened. Her cries to Jesus pierced our hearts: "Oh Lord, Oh Lord!" Mama cried out.

With tears, Joyce asked, "Mama, are you seeing Jesus?"

Mama responded, "He's the only one who can help me now."

With these cries, the tension and uncertainty of Mama's medical situation created a shroud, enveloping our hearts and every fiber of our beings with our own pain. When would the answers come? How would this end? No one could tell us anything with certainty, and time seemed to stand still even as the world spun around us, our hearts beating with doubt and fear.

As Mama's suffering increased, our hearts raced, and it was difficult for us to breathe; yet in the midst of all this spinning, one constant hugged our minds: Mama's faith. The same faith that had brought her through so much would bring her through this. *Surely He hears Mama crying out to Him, and surely He knows her faith.* Another miracle was nothing for God. In the midst of all this chaos, it was her cries to the Lord that gave us pause to stop and pray.

> *"Father," our hearts cried, "into your hands, we give this. You know our hearts, our love for our Mother. You know her love and faithfulness to you. We need your presence around us, keeping her strong and keeping us strong to be what our Mother needs us to be for her. We know we need another miracle, and we lay this request at your feet now. In Jesus' name we pray."*

With no money for a gift on Joyce's sixteenth birthday, Mama wrote her a poem and framed it with the only photo she had of herself and our father on their remarriage in 1970. In the poem she wrote, "Always remember, my bundle of love, no matter what, there is One above who can always make things right."

Our mother accepted Jesus in 1939 and was baptized and became a member of Greenlawn Baptist Church. She was fourteen when she took this step of faith and asked Jesus to be Lord of her life.

Over the years she attended or became a member of other churches depending on where she lived and her situation with transportation. Shortly before she died, she became a member of Holland Avenue Baptist Church, which she loved and attended together with our sister, Debbie. She so loved Pastor Charles Wilson, and he became such a blessing in those last few months, visiting her personally in her home and praying with her. His final visit to the hospital was just precious as he brought her the peace she needed to let go of this earthly existence. Just the sound of his voice and his beautiful prayer was a medley of soft music for her, and she began to relax in her faith, knowing she was going to her eternal destiny to walk in the sacred place with the Lord she loved so much.

God is good even when we may not see it at that moment. Mama's journey was not what she planned from the beginning, but when it was over, we learned from her last wishes and messages that she had lived her life the best she knew how and through the Lord, she was content. During those challenging years with our father, it was her faith and trust in the Lord that created the undercurrent that moved her forward. She assured us in her last words that we had a mother and a father who loved each other, and she wanted us to know we were born of that love. Her life held many complexities, and yet looking back now, we see her faith never wavered. It continued to carry her through life—the undercurrent that never ceased.

One of the beautiful things about Mama's faith was that she lived it by example while not always proclaiming it outwardly. Her faith was radiant! Her life was that of a simple woman with a servant's heart who loved the Lord and gave this life everything she had within her. She logged a lot of hours of labor and giving during those years. God can make a way for "the least of these" to impact others, and what God sees in us is all that matters.

We do recall a time when she had a particularly difficult financial situation and she half-laughingly said, "I know we have jewels and crowns waiting for us in heaven, but it sure would be nice to have a few down here right now."

In many ways, Mama's faith seemed to always be on autopilot. It was just a given in her life. But there were times when she was deeply challenged, needing to lean more on God. When our father passed away, it was one of the saddest times of Mama's life, but she trusted God to pull her through. When her son was on the ground in Vietnam, and she dealt with the same fears as she had when our father was engaged in battle in WWII, she leaned more on God during those times. When she got the news that her brother had passed away far too soon, she leaned on the Lord to pull her through. In those very lean times when she was not sure her children would even have food on the table or if they would be kept safe, she leaned more on God.

Mama was a faithful servant of the Lord. We often think of serving the Lord as quoting Scriptures, preaching or serving within the walls of a church, but God needs us out in the field too, touching lives without necessarily uttering Scripture but loving with a heart, a smile and a hug to all who need it. For fifty-one solid years of volunteer work, Mama was the hands and feet of Jesus to countless lives. We will never know how many people Mama touched, but we know the Lord was pleased. Only He could have made a way for this to happen for a woman who didn't hold educational degrees or celebrity status, didn't drive a car or have a driver's license, and was herself one of the "least of these" with little financial means.

Mama nurtured, held hands, fed, hugged, spoke to and made thousands of people feel the love of Jesus through the passion He placed in her heart for veterans, children with special needs, senior citizens, prisoners and all the volunteers whose paths crossed hers. She believed in people. She had that loving touch, and she believed everyone had a purpose and that God had given them that purpose and talent to be used to give back to others.

Mama truly did love the Lord with all her soul. Even in the worst of times she never lost her faith. She loved hearing the gospel preached, and she had many favorite Scriptures. In her later years, she became an avid reader of the Bible, with her own personal daily studies. She had read and studied the entire Bible three times and was working on her fourth. She set aside at least two or more hours every afternoon to study His Word. We all knew that if we came by to visit and saw her through the window with her little white satin hair bonnet on in the living room or at the dining room table, she was studying the Word and praying and we would not disturb her.

For therein is the righteousness of God revealed from faith to faith: As it is written, the just shall live by faith.
Romans 1:17 KJV

The day before she was admitted to the hospital for the final time, she had attempted her Bible study time but was unable to complete it. Below are her notes from that day's study as she struggled to write and finish. Her final study …

> 4-25-13   Romans 16:
> ① Bible: "Sister Phoebe commended" "Greeting Roman Saints"
> "Avoid Divisive Persons" "Greet one another with a Holy Kiss"
> the Church of Christ greet you — We are on the wrong track if
> we are constantly asking ourselves "what's wrong with it?"
> That's a question for immature believers, not growing one —
> God wants us to focus on what's good, not on what might
> be bad — To God alone wise, be glory through Jesus Christ
> forever — Amen
> ② Bible — Ecclesiastes 4: ~~~~~~

---

*"A Bible that's falling apart usually
belongs to someone who isn't."*
Charles Hayden Spurgeon

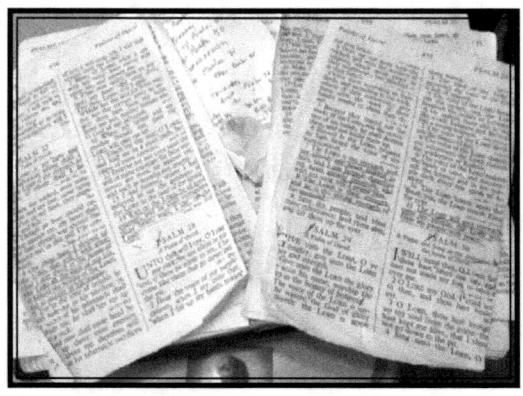

94   Letting Go

Joyce recently opened one of Mama's Bibles and a napkin fell out on which she had written her study notes in Psalms. As Joyce turned to the Psalms, the pages from this well-worn Bible sundered from the binding cascading across the table spilling out Scriptures she had underlined, and she obviously held close to her heart. Surely these were special to Mama on a daily basis. This was another discovery of her love for God's Word. It was gratifying to see her sweet handwriting and know her sweet hands had turned the pages of this book so many times that the binding was now falling apart! Mama was at peace with her life, especially in her later years, and she was at peace when the time came to accept she was going to go to her eternal home. She knew without a doubt when her last breath was breathed here that her next breath would be in heaven.

As we all get older, we realize we have many more years behind us than ahead of us. We are inching closer and closer to the door of heaven and our eternal home. Mama indeed grew hungrier to fill her soul with the Word of God.

A few years ago Bonnie created a little booklet of healing Scriptures which Mama faithfully read every day. It too is tattered now and has her special little underlines of the Scriptures she used to reinforce her mind with God's healing passages. On the back of the booklet, she underlined heavily, "I am going to walk by Faith."

Here are a few of Mama's favorite scriptures, perhaps these are some of your favorites too.

Though I speak with the tongues of men and of angels, and have not charity, I am become as sounding brass, or a tinkling cymbal. And though I have the gift of prophecy, and understand all mysteries, and all knowledge; and though I have all faith, so that I could remove mountains, and have not charity, I am nothing. And though I bestow all my goods to feed the poor, and though I give my body to be burned, and have not charity, it profiteth me nothing. Charity suffereth long, and is kind; charity envieth not; charity vaunteth not itself, is not puffed up, doth not behave itself unseemly, seeketh not her own, is not easily provoked, thinketh no evil; rejoiceth not in iniquity, but rejoiceth in the truth; beareth all things, believeth all things, hopeth all things, endureth all things. Charity never faileth: but whether there be prophecies, they shall fail; whether there be tongues, they shall cease; whether there be knowledge, it shall vanish away. For we know in part, and we prophesy in part. But when that which is perfect is come, then that which is in part shall be done away. When I was a child, I spake as a child, I understood as a child, I thought as a child: but when I became a man, I put away childish things. For now we see through a glass, darkly; but then face to face: now I know in part; but then shall I know even as also I am known. And now abideth faith, hope, charity, these three; but the greatest of these is charity.

1 Corinthians 13:1–13 KJV

The Lord is my shepherd, I shall not want.
He maketh me to lie down in green pastures:
he leadeth me beside the still waters. He restoreth my
soul: he leadeth me in the paths of righteousness for his
name's sake. Yea, though I walk through the valley of the
shadow of death, I will fear no evil: for thou art with me;
thy rod and thy staff they comfort me. Thou prepares a
table before me in the presence of mine enemies:
thou anointest my head with oil; my cup runneth over.
Surely goodness and mercy shall follow me all the days of
my life: and I will dwell in the house of the Lord forever.
Psalm 23 KJV

Make a joyful noise unto the Lord, all ye lands.
Serve the Lord with gladness: come before his presence
with singing. Know ye that the Lord he is God:
it is he that hath made us, and not we ourselves;
we are his people and the sheep of his pasture.
Enter into his gates with thanksgiving, and into
his courts with praise: be thankful unto him, and
bless his name. For the Lord is good; his mercy is
everlasting; and his truth endureth to all generations.
Psalm 100 KJV

> *I will lift up mine eyes unto the hills,*
> *from whence cometh my help. My help cometh from*
> *the Lord, which made heaven and earth. He will not*
> *suffer thy foot to be moved: he that keepeth thee will*
> *not slumber. Behold, he that keepeth Israel shall neither*
> *slumber nor sleep. The Lord is thy keeper: the Lord is*
> *thy shade upon thy right hand. The sun shall not smite*
> *thee by day, nor the moon by night. The Lord shall*
> *preserve thee from all evil: he shall preserve thy soul.*
> *The Lord shall preserve thy going out and thy coming*
> *in from this time forth, and even for evermore.*
> Psalm 121 KJV

You never know how strong your faith is until it is challenged beyond anything you could have ever imagined. Looking back now, we see how Mama's initial fear upon entering the ER moved into faith over the course of those hospital days. Her faith moved her to acceptance, and her acceptance moved her to the peace she needed to let go of this world and, harder yet, to let go of her children. Knowing how devastated we were going to be kept her pushing for healing till she just couldn't push anymore and she began letting go.

We learned new things about Mama on our quest to write this book. We discovered there were things we didn't know about because Mama never talked about them, including painful experiences of which she never spoke. She had obviously forgiven, made peace and let go of the pain.

We see Mama more clearly now that she is gone than we did when she was with us. When she was with us, we just saw

Mama. Seeing her now, she is so much more than our mom. She was a subtle soul and a faithful soul. She led a peaceful life in many ways and one full with purpose. She lived with courage and conviction. She was indeed a woman of strength. She is no longer just Mama to us, but a woman we admire for so many reasons we never saw before. Mama followed her passion in her volunteer work and followed her faith to her final destination in heaven. If there were one legacy she would want to leave, it would be that people turn their lives over to the Lord, find a bible believing church home, keep God as the center of their lives on a daily basis and live by His instructions.

We look back now and see that Mama slew many a giant in her lifetime. There were many times she could have given up on life, but she didn't. She slew unbelief when it would have been easy to fall prey to it. No matter what was going on, she never strayed from her faith or her principles. She could easily have done so, but she was not weak in that way. When she was down about the lack of money or food, especially when we were little, she trusted deep down inside that God would make a way, and He did. It may not have been a great bounty, but it was enough.

Not that I speak in respect of want: for I have learned, in whatsoever state I am, therewith to be content.
Philippians 4:11 KJV

When May 3rd was over and we had said goodbye, grief surely hit us hard. There was anger and, yes, even some anger toward God. And yet God allowed us our feelings, and He never left us. He didn't have to, but in His mighty way, He showed us the power of grace and the worthiness of the faith Mama put in Him all through the years. We look back now at all the signs He gave us, even in her passing, and see His love and mercy. Sometimes to see His glory, it takes getting this world out of our heads and getting His world into our heads. When we do, we see deeper into the meaning of this life and eternal life, our destiny in a place far beyond what our eyes can see and that we can only imagine. There were many subtle signs that day that God was with us then, and even now He is speaking to us: "I was with you then, and I am always with you."

---

*But you, LORD, are a shield around me,
my glory, the ONE who lifts my head high.*
Psalm 3:3 NIV

"With malice toward none, with charity for all, with firmness in the right as God gives us to see the right, let us strive on to finish the work we are in, to bind up the nation's wounds, to care for him who shall have borne the battle and for his widow and his orphan, to do all which may achieve and cherish a just and lasting peace among ourselves and with all nations."

Abraham Lincoln,
Second Inaugural Address
March 4, 1865

PART 3

Reaching

A Time to cast away stones, and a time to gather stones together; a time to embrace, and a time to refrain from embracing; A time to get, and a time to lose; a time to keep and a time to cast away.
Ecclesiastes 3:5-6 KJV

CHAPTER 6

Blessings through Miracles

*You are the God who performs miracles;
You display your power among the peoples.*
Psalm 77:14 NIV

Early that week in ICU, as the winds shifted and swirled around us, hearing one thing from one doctor, something else from another, and another thing yet again from the nurses, it was challenging to hold onto our faith and focus on healing. We wanted to believe for a miracle, but we could not even get definitive answers as to exactly what was wrong with Mama. We even heard, "She is very sick, but she is not dying." Of course, we wanted to cling to that as truth.

As the possible hub of infection shifted to her left shoulder, an X-ray was ordered. Aligned with the possibility of drawing what they thought was excessive fluid filled with infection from the shoulder, this new focus caused our hearts to spring into rejoicing and hope. We knew we were on the heels of

Mama's recovery. Surely it was God directing them to this shoulder to give her yet another miracle.

The intensity of this possibility was overwhelming, but it seemed it was taking forever to get the order. When you are riding the wave of hope, every passing hour seems like eternity. Determined to get things in motion, Debbie and Joyce walked over to Mama's physician's office and urged them to put a rush on it. Mama's doctor pushed the order through, and things started moving. Mama was then taken to X-ray so they could proceed to draw the infectious fluid from her shoulder.

But alas, the disheartening news came that there was very little fluid, and the shoulder was not the source of infection after all. Our hopes drained. Shortly afterward we saw our "guardian angel" nurse, Shanika, in the gift shop. Her face said it all.

As long as there was a thread of hope, we would hold onto it with all our might, but our hearts were waning. We refused to give up on Mama receiving another miracle. We were determined to stand strong in the face of this illness and to walk by faith, the same as Mama had always done.

Mama's life should have been over in 2001 after having a very serious heart attack. We knew something was amiss on that Friday morning, but Mama refused to go to the ER. Eventually, it was discovered that she'd had a heart attack in the wee hours of Friday morning, at which time she had been throwing up, in severe chest, arm and jaw pain. Her grandson,

Jason, had spent the night at her house and heard her. He got up to check on her. He asked her, "What's wrong, Grandma?"

She replied, "I am fine honey, go back to bed."

That Friday morning Bonnie dropped by to have coffee on her way to work, and Mama was drinking Milk of Magnesia and didn't look well. Bonnie asked, "Are you feeling okay?"

Mama responded, "I'm fine."

"Well, you don't look fine to me Mama. Are you sure?"

Mama responded firmly, "I am fine."

Bonnie was concerned so she called Joyce and asked her to go by and check on Mama because something wasn't right. Joyce immediately went to her house, and there stood Mama drinking water and baking soda.

When Joyce asked her what was wrong, Mama responded, "I just have a little heartburn. I am fine."

Joyce was not buying this and said, "I need to take you to the ER!"

Mama once again stated emphatically, "I am fine!"

Ironically, Mama attended a VA program, Because We Care Day, on that same Friday afternoon. Yep, that was Mama! She did not want to miss that program. Apparently, nothing, not even a heart attack, was going to keep her from serving those veterans.

How she managed to keep going after that heart attack is in itself a miracle. Mama was not improving, and she finally agreed to go to the ER Saturday morning. Guess what? She had actually had a very serious heart attack. She was immediately admitted, and a heart cath was performed. The news was not good—in fact, it was quite frightening. We were told there was a severe blockage in a major artery in the back of her heart. Due to the location of the blockage, there was nothing they could do. She was a walking time bomb. Good grief! Yea, she was "fine" alright!

We were shocked! And goodness, they were not compassionate at all when presenting this information—and saying it right in front of Mama. It was so matter-of-fact and cold as they basically told her to go home to die! Mama had many wonderful qualities, but she could be stubborn at times when it came to going to the doctor. She was not sick often, so she did not like her health to interfere with her plans. We were frustrated, and we fussed at her just as she would have fussed at us if we had ignored serious symptoms. In a loving, but firm way ... we let her know it too!

But as long as she was breathing, there was hope. We all immediately began to pray with great diligence and with healing Scriptures that it was not over for Mama. We prayed for God to intervene in this literal matter of the heart and give Mama more time.

Our prayers were answered in a very timely manner. Before releasing Mama, the cardiologist decided to run another test to get a better look at the blockage and damage to the heart. Upon returning to give us these results, he looked astonished at what he had just seen. To his amazement, the blockage had somehow cleared the artery, giving her another chance at life.

The cardiologist was totally in awe and told Mama she had received a miracle because he didn't know how this could have happened and she still be here. He said the heart had suffered damage, but while this artery could no longer help her, it could not harm her. Amazing! We praised God that Mama came home.

She dove right back into life with family and her volunteer work. She never ceased to amaze us! And being on this earth for seventy-six years, that's just the way she rolled.

How do you wash your feet? This was a question on the questionnaire on Mama's first doctor's visit after being diagnosed with diabetes in April of 1993. Joyce was helping her fill out the forms, and when she asked Mama how she washed her feet, Mama looked puzzled and laughed and said, "In the shower!" They both chuckled and after several more questions about feet and toes, realized there was a lot to learn about having diabetes! Mama was the first in our family to be diagnosed with it.

Mama dealt with the typical age-related health issues in her later years. She eventually dealt with the residual effects of diabetes, including peripheral neuropathy, making it difficult to wear shoes and Mama so loved pretty shoes! She didn't have many pairs, but she enjoyed the ones she had.

Thus a new mission began, and Bonnie and Mama set out to find shoes that fit her feet properly to help her foot and leg pain. Mama never liked wearing bedroom shoes outside her house, so the search for wearable shoes became an adventure, especially finding stylish diabetic ones. While her troubles never stopped her from finding joy in her life, finding the right shoes proved to be no simple matter! Sadly, they never accomplished this particular feat. No pun intended.

Then there was "Ol' Arthur," as she called it. She would talk to Ol' Arthur and tell him, "Ol' Arthur, you are not going to keep me down today!" She always said, "If you sit, you rust!" She seemed invincible at times and had such a great sense of humor!

Mama was determined to take advantage of every 'breath' and every 'step' God gave her, and that she did.

Every second spent with family or fulfilling her passion for volunteer work was worth whatever she had to endure. She was grateful for every precious moment. Most never knew her plight because she didn't talk about it. We often forgot what she was dealing with because of her silence and her determination to keep going.

My flesh and my heart may fail, but God is the strength of my heart and my portion forever.
Psalm 73:26 KJV

Mama always had a beautiful head of hair, but in those later years, like a lot of women, she began to lose her hair, particularly on top. Mama had one beautician the last twenty years of her life and, somehow, Janie could take twenty-six bobby pins and place that little hairpiece so securely on her head ... trust us, hurricane winds probably couldn't blow it off!

Mama became seriously ill with pneumonia in May 2011. She was hospitalized, and it was a touch-and-go situation. Having diabetes complicated things. Her blood sugars would spike with the steroids, and the breathing treatments could be torturous.

During Mama's bout with pneumonia, her doctor ordered a CT scan to make sure she did not have sinus issues that were adding to this stubborn, relentless illness. As sick as she was, she refused to remove that hairpiece. Well, off they took her to have the CT scan, and when she was wheeled back into the hospital room, the look on her face could have knocked a cowboy off his horse. In her hands, she held her little gray hairpiece and all twenty-six bobby pins. The hair piece had to be removed in order to do the scan. Needless to say, Janie was called to the hospital to perform the hairpiece rescue!

Mama's hair ... she was a faithful member of the "every week" beauty parlor club and her red lipstick, which also acted as her blush, was a must. We certainly didn't mind. If those two little things made her feel good about herself, then that was what she got.

Gray hair is a crown of splendor;
it is attained in the way of righteousness.
Proverbs 16:31 NIV

Once again God answered our prayers. It was truly another miracle. Through another tough season, Mama took the challenge, kept the faith and fought back with a vengeance. We praised God for yet another healing and Mama came home.

For I consider that the sufferings of this present
time are not worthy to be compared with
the glory which shall be revealed in us.
Romans 8:18 NKJV

And by His stripes we are healed.
Isaiah 53:5 NKJV

Later that year, Mama was diagnosed with a serious condition requiring surgery. At that point, Mama laughed and said: "This getting old business is for the birds. I've got things to do." She never saw her age as defining her as old. She was truly young at heart and mind.

She had developed an unsteady gait with tingling and numbness in her arms and hands. When Mama questioned her physician about these symptoms, her doctor had her perform some tasks to test her hand strength, and she tested poorly. To our shock, she was immediately sent to a neurosurgeon for further diagnosis. At age eighty-five, the word "neurosurgeon" was not what we wanted to hear! Deep breath!

Upon further evaluation and X-rays, Mama was diagnosed with cervical spinal stenosis. Her X-rays were scary. Surgery was her only option! Yes, surgery, on the spine—whoa! Your heart just falls to your feet when you hear the word *surgery*, much less on the spine!

Without the surgery, Mama ran the risk of complete loss of the use of her arms and hands and eventually paralysis. She was also at higher risk of falling, which could cause immediate paralysis. It was a scary place to be, and Mama was as terrified as we were.

Stronger healing prayers than ever began early as we prepared for the surgery. You have to understand that for many years Mama never even went to the doctor outside of regular checkups. She was always in reasonably good health and even bounced back from her heart attack and managed her diabetes well.

Two months passed before the surgery. It was critical that she prepare herself mentally and spiritually. Healing prayers had been going up diligently during this time as well as prayers for God to guide and bless the hands of the surgeon and all who would be with her in the operating room. Now Mama had to make the commitment to do this and set the surgery date. She definitely struggled with going through with this procedure.

And then an unexpected visit ...

One August night, Mama was sleeping soundly but awoke when she felt something gently tugging at her bedspread. She thought it was her son who was living with her at the time. Always a jokester, she wondered what in the world he was doing now! When this tugging didn't stop, she turned over; opening her eyes, and was astonished to see her father, who had passed away in 1980. He was sitting in a chair by the bed. He said to her, "Do you want to get well or keep having a pity party? Lizzie, are you going to keep feeling sorry for yourself, or do you want to get well?"

Our mother had absolutely no dementia, and she had a very clear mind. She knew what she saw and what she heard. Needless to say, she was taken aback! As she lay there, eyes wide open; she heard her mother's voice call out "Bob!" the name by which her mother called her father.

When she shared this with us, we asked if she had talked back to him, and she exclaimed "No way! I got out of that bed, cut on every light in the house and went into the den and turned on the TV!" We all had a good laugh over this, but we wished she had talked to him. We have all heard how loved ones who have passed on often begin to visit when someone's time is close at hand, so understandably, it was startling to her. But his message wasn't one of "it's your time," but rather one of, "Lizzie, go have the surgery, you will be okay!"

Finally, the day arrived for surgery. Prayers had been lifted without ceasing, and Mama was a fighter. As they prepped her for surgery, she asked us to go to the chapel and pray for her. Her surgeon also had prayer with her. That so blessed us, and Mama certainly welcomed it.

Three hours passed, and the surgeon came to gather us together. He said, "She did very well through the surgery, and I am very pleased, but the next 24 hours are critical."

We were very anxious to see her and talk to her. Other than being a little uncomfortable she was in good spirits. For some reason, the surgeon did not order a catheter, which meant she would have to walk herself to the restroom. We relied on hospital staff to help her, as we did not feel we knew how best to handle her since she just had major surgery on her neck and spine. We would also leave the room to give her privacy, which unfortunately proved to be a mistake.

When it seemed Mama would be fine, we decided we would take turns staying overnight with her. Joyce said she would take the first night. Unfortunately, Mama had to go to the restroom again, but this time, it would change the course of that hospital stay. Joyce left the room to give Mama privacy as usual. Then Joyce saw the nurse run out of the room, so she went in to check on Mama and found her still in the restroom. Her pain had become intolerable, and her body began shaking uncontrollably. Panic began to set in, and by the time she was helped back into the bed, her heart rate had dropped to thirty. Ironically, Joyce found out that those she thought were helping Mama off the bed and to the restroom were making her pull herself up off the bed. This put way too much pressure on her neck.

Joyce had the nurse call the hospital's emergency response team. Yes, you read that right, Joyce had the nurse call the emergency response team, and they arrived in what seemed like seconds. To Joyce, it was like something from a TV episode, and her own heart was racing. The medic questioned

Mama about pain and shortness of breath, and she calmly stated, "No. Is everything ok?" After quickly evaluating Mama, the medic dialed Intermediate ICU where she was moved immediately so she could be closely monitored and receive better oversight and care.

Joyce called everyone back to the hospital as Mama's heart rate would not come back up. Oddly, Mama seemed unaffected by what was happening, other than the severe pain she was experiencing, but she was in a very serious situation.

It was way past midnight at this point, and the family had returned to be with Mama. As we entered her room, we stood amazed as outside her window was the beautiful sight of a cross atop the steeple of a church. The light from the moon shone upon it. How awesome this was, as Mama could see it from her bed. How calming it was to know God was there.

The beautiful cross outside the hospital window gave us peace.

At this time, a wonderful nurse, Jonathan, began taking care of Mama. While Mama was not comfortable with male nurses, she grew to love Jonathan and eventually only wanted him at her side. We will forever be grateful to him.

It was nine long days and nights in the IICU. During that time, those machines would ping and pong, and it was such a blessing when they would turn the sound off in the room. How nerve-wracking the sounds were! And how long the nights seemed when the hospital staff was smaller, and everything was quiet except the sounds of those machines and the light chatter amongst the staff.

There were a couple of times Mama seemed oddly unaffected by her low heart rate and unstable blood pressure. We recall one time she was sitting up eating a little lunch, and her heart rate kept dropping back to the thirties. Jonathan was on call, and he came rushing into the room as he was closely monitoring her at the nurses' station and asked her if she had any chest pains.

She replied, "No."

Jonathan asked, "Are you having any shortness of breath?"

Mama replied, "No."

All the while she was eating her lunch like nothing was going on! We all looked at each other in astonishment and disbelief. Her heart and blood pressure was clearly out of range during this time, and yet she seemed unaffected.

The hospital became our home away from home. Fortunately, this hospital had a great waiting room with a number of TVs and chairs you could make into your own little private corner to get some rest and get away from the sounds of the machines and the anxiety in Mama's room. It was a place where you could pray and praise God away from all the noise, especially at night.

Mama's heart would not stabilize, so she needed a pacemaker and once placed, she greatly improved. Through all these days, we were constantly reminded of God's love and grace. He had placed us in this particular room where the vision of that beautiful cross stood like a light high on the church steeple, showing up even more brilliantly in the middle of those long nights, bringing us hope. Through it all, God gave Mama yet another miracle healing. Her father's words had come to pass. She made it through the surgery and, once again, Mama came home.

The holiday season was upon us now, and our family was filled to the brim with blessings. We enjoyed Mama's side dishes of warm cornbread dressing, the best potato salad, deviled eggs, and her turkey…simply mouthwatering for our Thanksgiving celebration. She was feeling great!

However, the next day the surgical tape over Mama's pacemaker incision came off and to our dismay, it appeared to be infected. Shocked—off we went to the ER. If the infection moved inside the pocket, the pacemaker would have to come out, and that would be that! There was also a little hole in the incision, creating a clear opening down into the pocket. Somehow the staples had not closed the entire incision.

This was so concerning that the emergency room doctor contacted Mama's cardiologist who had placed the pacemaker. The ER doctor prescribed antibiotics and gave us cleaning instructions. Early Monday morning we met with her cardiologist. He was very concerned and said we really needed a miracle. He stated it looked like the infection was just in the incision for the time being, but the hole was very troubling as he had never seen this happen before. He had been thinking about Mama all weekend, ever since the ER doctor called him, praying it would be okay when he saw her. It was clear by the look on his face that the situation was serious. We held on to the good news that the infection didn't seem to have moved into the pocket … yet. We kept God very busy with healing requests during that time.

Loaded with more antibiotics and a strict cleaning regimen, we headed home. By mid-January the following year, the incision had finally closed and healed, although Mama would stay on antibiotics a while longer. Praise be to God for yet another healing!

---

*For I will restore health unto thee,
and I will heal thee of thy wounds, saith the LORD...*
Jeremiah 30:17 KJV

Through this new season of being there for Mama in her senior years, we drew even closer to her and to one another, and our admiration for her strength was reinforced. She was always amazing as she went through these medical ordeals. She definitely was a fighter. No matter the level of pain, she pushed through. She lived her life full-out in her later years, just as she did in her younger years.

Mama wrapped her hair in toilet paper every night. Her hair had to last a week between hair appointments. It was not unusual for us to see her like this as she had done this routine every night since we could remember. Each night when Mama wrapped her hair in toilet paper, she put on her pretty white satin and lace bonnet before going to bed. And you never messed with that bonnet or that routine. In fact, she had to have a particular bonnet, which could only be found at one store. No other style would do. This was another way Mama rolled. Certain things were not going to change.

When Mama was in rehab after her first hip surgery, her roommate was Mrs. Owens, a cool lady who had served our country. One night after we helped Mama change into her PJs, we wheeled her out of the bathroom and, as Mrs. Owens was sitting there talking to us, Mama asked for the toilet paper. We thought nothing of this ritual. Mama wrapped her hair and then put on her bonnet, and we helped her into bed. With her favorite soft-foam white neck pillow in place, she settled in for the night. To our surprise, Mrs. Owens said, "I've never seen anyone do that, nor have I seen anyone look that beautiful going to bed. She looks like a queen!"

We all burst out laughing, and from then on, Mama's nickname was "The Queen." Mrs. Owens became such a special friend and, even after Mama's passing, we visited her regularly and fell in love with her. We lost Mrs. Owens in August 2014. God certainly blessed us with this precious relationship. It gives us comfort to know that she and 'The Queen' are having a blast in heaven! What a blessing when God allows our paths to cross with other people who become special to us!

We grew so used to miracle healings that we came to expect them. Fast-forward to April 26, 2013. Mama had just survived two hip surgeries by the grace of God, so why would this time be any different? Mama had plenty of living yet to fulfill. But as that last week of her illness progressed, we knew without a doubt our mama would not want to live with permanent PIC lines for IV antibiotics and being unable to walk. A different kind of miracle awaited both Mama and us. It was so disappointing that Mama had fallen on that cold December day and fractured her hip, but it had happened, and no one could change that.

Even during her battle those last four months, she made sure the monthly program was continued at the VA Hospital. In February of 2013, she was determined to go to the AMVETS Valentine's Day program. As challenging as it was, we helped her dress and off we went to the VA with her and her wheelchair. Fortunately, she had a great AMVETS team, and everything was wonderful as usual. Even in all her pain, she found joy in being able to be there.

That day a very special lady, Diane Rainey, the recreational assistant at the VA Hospital, presented Mama with a beautiful red afghan made by the patients. We were told later that the patients kept asking when the lady with the good sandwiches and bingo money was coming back. That visit became a very precious memory in our hearts. The pictures we took that day have become the most cherished that we have of Mama. And she was wearing her little angel pin! We love having this in a photograph. Mama loved collecting angels, and she wore one every day.

Mama was excited to attend a banquet in April held at the VA Hospital to honor the volunteers. She won a door prize! The first time ever! It was a beautiful set of miniature candles, and she was thrilled. How could we have known that this would be her last event at the VA Hospital? The very next week she so wanted to go to the VA Hospital BINGO program and tried to go, but she just couldn't. That was on a Thursday, and by Friday night she would be admitted to the hospital for the final lap of her race.

Mama was a fighter, but she had been giving out since her fall. The previous four months had been hard on her body. We still held out for a miracle. Mama always came home! Always! But this time, Mama was going to a different home. She was about to complete the ultimate goal that had been set so many years ago. The final checkmark was about to be placed.

I have set the Lord always before me: because he is at my right Hand, I shall not be moved.
Psalm 16:8 KJV

We strive so much for miracles of healing that sometimes we forget the greatest healing of all is only complete when we finish our journey here and enter the gates of eternal life with Jesus. Of course, it is natural and normal to pray and desire healing for a longer journey here with our loved ones. And we should desire and have faith in those promises of healing. Why some are healed, and others are not, is unknown and can be challenging to deal with, but we have to trust that God knows best.

God's will can be quite difficult to grasp when you are in the storm, yet somehow deep within our souls, this truth exists. Life is a blessing, but we sometimes forget life is also eternal and when it is time for the body to release the soul, the person lives on in a far greater and most glorious place.

When we realized God was ready for Mama to come home, there was indeed great sadness. To some, that may seem selfish, as Mama had lived a long life, but to us, it was natural to feel that way. We had such a history with her. We loved her deeply, and we wanted more time with her.

Anger would come and go in the following months, and we all had some harsh conversations with God, but we always knew deep down that God knew what was best for our mother. He had given us miracle healings and more time with her every time we asked, but this time, He wasn't going to answer our way. We were reminded of 1 Peter 5:10 (ESV): *"And after you have suffered a little while, the God of all grace, who has called you to his eternal glory in Christ, will himself restore, confirm, strengthen, and establish you."*

CHAPTER 7

The Silver Cord is Loosed

> *Or ever the silver cord be loosed,*
> *or the golden bowl be broken, or the pitcher be broken*
> *at the fountain, or the wheel broken at the cistern.*
> *Then shall the dust return to the earth as it was:*
> *and the spirit shall return unto God who gave it.*
> Ecclesiastes 12:6–7 KJV

Little did we know our mother's last week of her life was about to begin. Nor did we realize the pain she would endure, the confusion that would surround her illness and the agony of no real answers for what was happening. Many of you have been there also.

Saturday, December 22nd, the day Mama fell and fractured her hip, she was rushing about preparing for Christmas so she could go visit her grandson Jason, who was in IICU at the hospital. She slipped on some water on the floor by the washing machine and took a fall. She ended up in one tower of the hospital with her grandson in another tower. We never dreamed this was our last Christmas with our mother.

We would not be eating that good ole' southern fried chicken and grits this Christmas morning, a tradition we all looked forward to. Only Mama could cook grits and fried chicken that were drool-worthy.

It's the morning of Christmas Eve. The hospital was unusually quiet, with a skeleton crew. Mama was being prepped to have three screws implanted in her hip. Time passed ever so slowly while sitting in the waiting room, walking about the waiting room, sitting again and watching the screen that reports what point the patient is in during surgery, all the while praying.

The lobby was decorated beautifully with Christmas trees and almost life-sized carolers. It appeared they were there just for us and yet, in all the silence, they were haunting in a strange way. We were reminded of it being the day before we celebrated Jesus's birthday, and we prayed Mom would come through this surgery to celebrate that day, even if it would be in the hospital.

Suddenly, the door opened, and the doctor approached. She had done very well in surgery, and we could see her soon. How thankful our hearts were that she came through well, and we looked up and said: "Thank you, Lord!"

Soon she was up walking with a walker and, while her pain level was high, it was manageable. There was some debate as to whether to do in-home therapy or send her to a rehab facility. Reluctantly, the decision was made for her to go to a rehab facility, a decision we would come to regret.

Mama would spend the next four weeks in a rehab facility where her therapy was so aggressive that it eventually caused an ER visit. We did not know the extent of the damage done until March when Mama would have to endure a second surgery to receive a partial hip implant.

The first three days she could get up and walk very well, but the aggressive therapy in rehab began to take its toll. Her pain became unbearable to the point she sometimes had to have therapy from her bed. This was very disturbing, and we continuously questioned the staff about the therapy being too aggressive. They said she needed it. We asked, "What good is it to tear up her arthritic knees and her feet to do therapy for hip surgery?" There was nothing to gain except damage. After nine days, Mama had an unexplained and serious episode that sent her to the ER.

The morning she went to the emergency room she was due to go to an appointment with her surgeon, and we were planning to ask him about taking her home for in-home therapy. We told Mama the night before her appointment with her surgeon not to let the staff get her up and take her to therapy.

Upon arriving around 7:30 a.m., Bonnie found Mama in the occupational therapy room exercising her arms. You see, Mama always felt compelled to cooperate, but this was very upsetting as Mama's left shoulder had already been hurting. Bonnie took her back to her room and helped her into bed. She was in severe pain all over, including her arms and left shoulder. From there she went to not feeling her legs, and then she said she was losing her sight.

Bonnie ran for the nurse, who came and checked Mama's vitals and the nurse said she was fine. But Mama was clearly panicking, and so was Bonnie. Frustrated and fearful, Bonnie called Joyce and told her she was needed and to hurry as she could not get the nurse to come back to assist with Mama. In the meantime, Mama started throwing up violently. One of the aides was so sweet and came in to help. We tried to get the nurse to call the facility doctor, but she said the doctor was not due to come to the facility today, and Mama's vitals were fine. Mama was clearly not fine.

Joyce called Mama's surgeon, who said to take her to the emergency room. Unable to move her, we called for an ambulance. She was clearly in major distress. In the emergency room, they gave her IV pain meds and something to relax her. They kept her for a while, but they never determined a diagnosis. They just documented that she was throwing up and having an anxiety attack. Really? Now we wonder, could this have been the beginning of the bacterial infection that eventually took such a high toll?

We missed the surgeon's appointment because of that episode, and he didn't bother to come and check on her at the hospital. She had to go back to the rehab facility. We didn't know what to do. She was on some very expensive blood-thinning injections, at the cost of around $500 a day. If we took her home, we would have to pay out of pocket for them—at least that is what we were told.

> *Always be a voice for your loved one! We regret we did not instruct the staff ourselves that Mama was not to do any therapy until after her doctor's appointment.*

Mama's pain would continue to get worse, and we continued to question and fight against therapy that was clearly doing more harm than good, as she became less and less mobile. Through all this, we were still being told her pain level was normal at this stage. But now Mama could barely walk, and they continued to push two and a half hours a day of aggressive therapy on her, like riding a bicycle and standing on her tiptoes. Really? She was eighty-seven years old and rarely complained, but she just couldn't do it. Yet she tried so hard to do what she thought was needed to help her heal. Sadly, it was killing her. It was a continuous battle as more and more days of therapy would have to be done from her bed, which was also excruciating. It was a nightmare.

The day finally came when we could take Mama home and start in-home therapy and nursing assistance. While it was so much better, it seemed the damage had been done, as her pain was still great and getting worse, and she just wasn't improving. Although we kept calling the surgeon's office to inquire about Mama's pain, they kept insisting it was normal. It was heartbreaking to see her struggle with unbearable pain that was supposedly normal.

On Thursday, March 7, 2013, the time came to go back to the surgeon. This time, we wanted answers about the pain and Mama's lack of progress. X-rays were taken. The doctor walked back into the room and jumped up to sit on the patient table and shared the news ... the pins had moved through the bone! What? We were shocked and dismayed! We were also shocked and dismayed at the surgeon's nonchalant attitude about it. Mama was in a wheelchair with a pain level way past ten, and he said she would need to decide if she could live with this pain or have another surgery. Really? Did he honestly think she could live with this level of pain, and also with a broken bone apparently still in her body? Good grief!

Of course, Mama was petrified at the thought of another surgery and said she would like to think and pray about it. I think we were all numb at this point. Joyce wanted to go back and ask to see the X-rays, but Mama just wanted to go home. As her daughters, we felt that the doctor should have sent her straight to the hospital and scheduled her for surgery. Mama would have accepted that. But instead, we went home speechless, numb and sick.

The next morning Mama was completely immobile and in agonizing pain. It was frightening. We called 911 for an ambulance. *Oh my gosh*, we thought, *how will she handle a ride to the hospital in this much pain?* When the ambulance arrived, Joyce was relieved to find she knew one of the paramedics. When Timmy came through the door, we knew God was with us. As the paramedics moved her from her bed to the stretcher Mama cried and hollered out in pain, and it tore us apart. We had never heard our mother cry out like this. Our hearts were aching knowing she had to endure this ride. She had been through so much, and we had battled for her as best we knew how, and now here we were.

We followed the ambulance to the hospital. With every bump in the road, we felt for Mama and the tears flowed. We knew they were doing everything they could to make the ride as painless for her as possible. It was such a helpless feeling. Was Mama even going to make it through this ride to the hospital?

Mama was admitted, and the surgeon on call performed surgery for a partial hip replacement. She did great! Yes, another miracle! She was walking well the next day, and the pain was greatly reduced. It was a new day! We decided to do in-home therapy from the start this time, and Mama breezed through therapy the next few weeks. Mama felt she could take on the world again! At eighty-seven, she still had a lot to do, and we were all so happy that her pain had become manageable. But our excitement would not last long, as something unexpected was going on within Mama's body that would not be found until it was too late.

March 20th was Mama's first visit back to the surgeon. Using her walker, she walked with her head held high and with ease all the way from the car to his office and actually sat in a chair in the waiting area. You do not know the gift of sitting in a chair or even putting on socks and shoes until you can't do it. During this journey, we learned to greatly appreciate these gifts in life. The doctor removed her sutures and was very happy with her progress. He told her there was a one percent chance of infection with this type of implant, and he told her, "Mrs. Glenn, you are good to go."

We left on that famous cloud nine … we had our mama back, and she was going home. If she could have, we believe Mama would have hitch-kicked her way out of the doctor's office. She was so grateful for all the blessings she had received. We thought we were on our way to her having a full recovery.

A month later, on Thursday, April 18, 2013, Mama was given final clearance by her surgeon and her physical therapist. That Thursday Mama had also been to her beautician and gone out to eat lunch, which she had not been able to do since the first surgery back in December. It was a celebratory day! The next day she attended an AMVETS luncheon at the VA Hospital, where she won her first door prize of beautiful candles, and she was excited. Nothing could have caught us more off guard than what was about to come down the pipeline.

On Saturday, April 20, 2013, Joyce had lunch with Mama, and all seemed well. That evening, however, Debbie came by and found Mama in a very deep sleep. Even more curious was the fact that she was lying flat on the bed, which she *never* did. She joked about it the next evening, stating, "I think I scared Debbie last night. She came to ask me to go eat, and she tried to wake me up. She thought I was in a coma because

I was sleeping so hard." Although this was concerning to us, Mama insisted she was fine.

On Sunday morning, Mama was adamant that she was going to go to church. She and Debbie enjoyed a wonderful service, and everyone at church told her how beautiful she looked. She had lunch at a seafood restaurant she hadn't been to in a long time. Overall, Mama had a very good day.

Sunday afternoon, Bonnie came by with yet another pair of shoes she had ordered for Mama to try on. Mama didn't want to do that right then, so Bonnie left them and said she could just try them on when she came back the next day. Sadly, Mama never would wear that pair of shoes, and Bonnie still has them in her keepsake memory chest.

Monday began the last leg of Mama's earthly race. Joyce arrived at Mama's house about 8:15 a.m. to find her sick to her stomach. Joyce asked if she thought her nausea medicine would help, and it worked well enough that Mama ate a little breakfast. Being diabetic, she needed to eat. Then she wanted to go back to bed and rest. Going in to check on her later, Joyce found her once again lying flat and sound asleep. Her cheeks were blood red, and Joyce decided to wake her to take her temperature, which was 102°. This was alarming. We tried to convince her to go to her own doctor, but she kept saying that her office was closed on Mondays. Now Mama had absolutely no dementia, so this statement did give us cause for concern. She'd had a fever, so we related her confusion to that. Eventually, we were able to get her up and to the emergency room. She was shaking and having terrible chills.

We arrived at the ER at 2:00 p.m. and told them her symptoms, and they took her vitals. They put an IV in and drew some blood. Two hours later we were still sitting in the lobby. She had begun to shake so badly that we asked for a blanket. They would not give us a warm blanket because her fever had broken and they said it might give her a fever again. After another hour of waiting, Mama was shaking so badly she was drooping down into her wheelchair. We went to the desk to see if she could be seen immediately, or at least lie down somewhere, as she could not sit there like that any longer. We were ignored.

It was decided that Joyce would to go to a nearby medical facility and explain what was happening. They said that they could see her.

When we arrived, they took her back immediately. We questioned twice whether she might be dehydrated, but they felt she wasn't. They did a urinalysis and blood work. Her blood pressure was a little low, and she still had the shakes, chills, and extreme thirst. Nothing showed up in her blood work. They did x-rays of her back and stomach … nothing. She was tested for the flu … still nothing. They decided that she must have a virus. It was incredible to us. All those terrible symptoms and nothing! We did wonder if she had an infection since she'd had two surgeries so close together, but they did not think that was the case as she had no hip pain—the pain was in her back, left shoulder, and neck.

Mama already had a doctor appointment the next day with her regular physician, so we took her home. At home that night she was actually able to eat something, and she felt a little better and had no fever. The next day at her physician's visit, we informed her doctor of what had taken place on Monday and described her symptoms. Had she still been running a fever, we would have been sent to the hospital, but, unfortunately, that was not the case. However, her blood pressure was low which we questioned. We were confused as no infection had shown up in her blood work the night before. At that point, we were given no medical reason to believe it was anything other than a virus and would run its course. Later that day, out of the blue, Mama commented that it was her Mother's birthday today and she had died three days later on April 26th - the date Mama would be admitted to the hospital for her final leg of this earthly race.

Months later, Joyce went back to the medical facility that had seen Mama on that Monday night and asked for Mama's medical records from that visit. She was shocked to see beneath her lab work, FLAGS: lymphopenia, granulocytosis, and macrocytosis. This information had not been relayed to us that night. Perhaps had we known about these flags, which indicated infections and low immune system, we would have taken these indicators to Mom's regular doctor the next day. Could it have possibly made a difference? This is burned in our memories even today.

Mama had a good day Wednesday. She ate well. She was out-of-the-ordinary cranky that morning, but later she was up and adamantly insisted the Christmas tree, now turned Easter tree, be taken down. She and Bonnie spent the day taking her tree down and packing it up. She ate a great lunch and was able to complete a long Bible study, which she thoroughly enjoyed. She was insistent about mailing a donation she wanted to make to the Paralyzed Veterans Organization. She wanted it mailed that day, so Bonnie took it to the post office right away.

Later, Bonnie and Mama were watching TV and talking, and Mama looked down at a magazine cover that had a picture of Valerie Harper on it. Mama commented on her, and they talked about how much they had always liked her. They discussed her battle with brain cancer and Bonnie commented to Mama, "At least we aren't dealing with anything terminal"— but Mama was silent. Bonnie's heart fell, and a sick feeling came over her as there was something about that silence that screamed something dreadful was about to happen.

However, Mama did have a good evening, and she even sat up voting by phone for Candice Glover on *American Idol*. She wanted Candice to win, so she voted over and over again.

On Thursday, Mama so wanted to go to the VA Hospital program, but she was not able. Her neck was stiff and hurting, and she could not raise her left arm. Her legs and feet were hurting too. She thought she had pulled something in her back while reaching for the TV remote. She did sit up on the side of her bed and eat a good, healthy lunch. She later tried to get up and have her daily Bible study, but she was only able to do a short one. We tried compresses and Biofreeze on her neck. She was tired and hurting and wanted to go back to bed and rest. She took some Aleve and began to feel somewhat better. She did not want to go to the ER, and she did okay throughout the night.

Sadly, Friday morning she began to run a fever again. She was completely miserable. We called her doctor who told us to take her to the ER. The downward spiral now begins ...

Unbeknownst to us, the horror of a bacterial infection and sepsis had taken hold. Nobody had caught it because it does not show up in regular blood work. We would later learn that it is only found through a blood culture. Why this wasn't done earlier, since after the fact we learned that Mama had the typical symptoms of a bacterial infection, we do not know. This continually haunts us today because we now know the earlier it is detected, the better chance of survival.

The caterpillar to butterfly becomes so symbolic when a loved one returns home to the Creator. The butterfly's metamorphosis is such a beautiful natural event. This amazing phenomenon is reflective of our souls, which are cocooned in our physical bodies. But for the soul to be set free to live on, the physical body must die and release it. Reflecting back, we see a pattern of events that unfolded during the last days before Mama began showing signs of illness, signs that she was getting ready to fly from her cocoon. However, we were not prepared for what was coming.

Two weeks before Mama's passing, her hairdresser Janie had recently opened her new salon, and Mama was bound and determined to enjoy the whole hair experience. No matter what, she was going to lie back in that chair and let Janie wash her hair, something she had not yet been able to do since her fall four months earlier. She wanted to attend church and eat at one of her favorite restaurants. She made a donation to the Paralyzed Veterans Organization and insisted it be mailed that day. A poster adorned with healing scriptures and messages from family and friends hung in her bedroom, and she decided to take it down.

Although these things seemed insignificant at the time, after Mama passed, they seemed to have meant something more. Was she subconsciously letting go and separating from this earthly life? We have come to believe that yes, she was.

One of the hardest realities for us to embrace was learning that all her symptoms were clearly those of someone with a bacterial infection for which she was at high risk. Yet no one earlier in the week had pursued a blood culture. We all had to come to terms that if she had been treated earlier in that week, maybe she could have had a very different outcome. It was difficult to find peace with that, especially since her suffering and pain were so great in that last week. The destruction it did to her body, and the neurological damage were horrific.

Through it all, we know without a doubt that God was always with us. We thanked God for allowing us to be human and for understanding when we were hurting. We were most grateful to Him for never letting go of our hands, when we are hanging by a thread, and for reminding us that even through the most difficult storms in life, "all things work together for good to them that love the Lord, to them that are the called according to His purpose" (Romans 8:28).

Mama as a young girl

Daddy handsome in his uniform

The shed we stayed in for a while

Joyce, Debbie & Bonnie excited about our Christmas gift!

Lockwood and Daddy in 1968

Daddy in 1969 on the road to recovery

Our beautiful Mother

Debbie, Lockwood, & Bonnie

Mama, Debbie, Bonnie, Joyce, Jason and Brittany Christmas 1984

Mama and some precious AMVET ladies enjoying a Hawaiian Luau! Always a fun time to be had with these ladies

Mama and another AMVET lady dressed as clowns!

Mama preparing for a trip to Miracle Hill ... always working

Veteran of the Month!

Mama with her father after crowning him King for a Day!

Joyce Wagster & Bonnie Jennings

Danyele Browder Gardner and Mama ... A great day was had at the VA Hospital!

*Mama's last trip to the National AMVETS Convention ...
Orlando, Florida in August 2012
Mary, Mama, Wanda*

Mama, Kim Aiken Cockerham, and Mary on the road to Miss America

Hayden and Taylor enjoying ice cream in the cafeteria of the hospital Christmas 2012 ... their dad in one tower of the hospital with their Maw Maw in another tower! Making the best of having Christmas in the hospital

Irene, Mama, Helen and Joyce ... Sisters enjoying a good time in 2010

*Getting ready for Christmas at the VA Hospital 2012
a few days before Mama would fall and fracture her hip!
Mama, Joyce, Regina, Diane, and Mary*

*Glenda Browder and Mama at
her 80th birthday celebration!*

*Mama's little Min Pin
doggie, Little Moe*

Mama after her second surgery in the waiting room of her surgeon's office...when we thought she was on her way to a full recovery! So happy to see her sitting and in very little pain at this time!

Mama in 2005 on her 80th birthday!

Maw Maw and grandson Bradley

Maw Maw and grandson Brandon

CHAPTER 8

Becoming Silent

*Whereas you do not know what will happen tomorrow.
For what is your life? Is it even a vapor that appears
for a little time and then vanishes away.*
James 4:14 NKJV

"I want to go to the beach." That would be one of the last coherent statements spoken by our precious mother on that Friday, April 26th, while we waited with her in the ER. Joyce had plans to go to the beach the week of May 18th and had planned to take Mama for a couple of days, not only to see the ocean but to visit her grandson, Brandon, and his wife, Hannah, in their new apartment and attend one of their magic performances. But this plan would never be realized.

Mama spent half a day in the ER with all kinds of tests being run: CT scans, EEGs, EKGs, x-rays and a blood culture. Mama's neck and left arm were in extreme pain, and she was unable to move her neck. Our hearts were sinking, but we were still hopeful she would beat this.

It was finally decided she would be admitted. We found out the next week that they had seriously considered sending her home since all her tests were normal. We would have never allowed this as it was our fourth time trying to find out what was going on with her!

Mama had a really hard night. The moans coming from Mama were becoming worse and worse, and she began to repeatedly cry out, "Oh Lord. Oh Lord!"

Joyce asked, "Mama are you seeing Jesus?"

Mama responded, "He's the only one who can help me now!"

A long night began of holding Mama's hand, putting warm compresses on her body, contacting family and praying. This was not our mama, and the pain medicine was not helping. We had no idea what was happening but knew something had taken over our sweet mother, and we were scared.

At 5:00 a.m. on Saturday morning, two nurses came running in with bags of medicine saying, "She has a bacterial infection, and we have to act fast!" The blood culture results had been read, and they needed to begin antibiotics immediately.

Then came the catheterization! It's hard to even go there. This procedure hurt her so badly and our precious mother, who rarely complained even with her arthritis and diabetic neuropathy, cried out in agony, "Please get me out of here and take me home!"

Joyce noticed they were bending her leg and pressing down on the hip where she had just had surgery! It was obviously very painful, and Joyce firmly told the nurse, "Please do not do that! That is her bad hip, and she just had two surgeries on that hip!"

Mama cried and moaned, something we had never witnessed her doing even through all the struggles of her life, and we were helpless to make it better.

With everything going on, the nurse did not tell us anything about what a bacterial infection could mean. While Mama was crying out, we were trying to soothe her and help her through this.

That afternoon Mama's kidneys began to fail, and the kidney specialist said he needed to move her to ICU to administer medication to get them functioning again. He let us know she was not being moved to ICU for the infection, but to kick-start her kidneys. Still, we had no idea what we were dealing with. We were relieved for her to go to ICU because we knew she would be taken care of more closely and we could get more answers.

During the course of these events, Mama lost her ability to speak. She could only attempt with gestures to tell us what was wrong. She could nod her head. She had never cried like this before.

The wide-eyed look of fear on her face at that time will continue to haunt us. It was truly heartbreaking and all just so unexpected. We were dismayed at how we had gotten here in the first place when we tried earlier in the week to get her help and a proper diagnosis. We asked questions but received no clear answers. What kind of bacterial infection did she have? Finally, we were told it was a staph infection that she could have picked up from anywhere, or it could have come from the surgeries.

We were deeply shocked and heartbroken at the turn of events. Yes, she was eighty-seven—we get that! But Mama's life force and love for life, people, and God were huge. She was our rock, and it was extremely difficult to watch her suffer.

Mama was a fighter, but she was tired – emotionally and physically. She had fought a good fight since that fall in December; she really had. How she had endured so much pain and two hip surgeries and still tried to keep going is a testament to her faith, her life force, and her strong will. Our family, heartbroken at the reality we were now facing, would take a long time to come to terms with everything that had happened to her in the last four months of her life.

On Monday morning, April 29th, we were graced with the presence of Mama's new ICU nurse, Shanika. We knew from the moment we met her that she was special. When she walked into the ICU room, there was an essence of peace about her, and she treated our mother as if she were her own. Yes, this was her job, but her compassion and sincerity were so evident, and we knew Mama was in the hands of someone God had placed in our paths and someone we would never forget.

Mama began crying out again. Not being able to understand her communication with us was causing her to drift farther and farther away, breaking us down too. During this moment of obvious suffering, trying to figure out what she was trying to communicate, Joyce asked her if she was nauseated and, with great struggling, using all her strength and effort, Mama managed to yell out, "Yes!"

We went to Shanika, and she immediately took care of the situation, which helped Mama so much to calm down and rest. It wasn't just Shanika doing what needed to be done that made a difference; it was that she did it in a way that made it personal and not just routine duty. She was professional, yet had such a personal element to her work, unifying her skills and compassion completely. She created an environment that said, "I am not just here for your mother, but for the family too."

Shanika's gifted ability to care for our mother with this added loving touch greatly impacted our mother's care and our need to know that Mama was seen as a person and not just a patient. Shanika was a blessing amidst all the mystery and frustration of Mama's illness and we will always remember her as our guardian angel.

Although we were told in the ICU that Mama was not dying, she was still very sick and needed a lot of care. We were warned that the medicines would make her loopy and she would be out of it. It was also good for her to yell out some, as it would keep her lungs expanded. We all prayed so hard; the one thing no one ever wants for a loved one is for them to suffer. Mama was clearly suffering in many ways, and it was overwhelming.

She had screamed out a couple of times for us to get her out of there! She also called out to her deceased sister while reaching upward with her right arm, "Irene, please come help me!" We had never seen our mother like this. Our hearts continued to break as Mama did not even look like herself anymore. What was really happening here? How had all this happened when a few days earlier we had been celebrating? Yet, here we were. It was real and surreal at the same time.

Joyce went to the hospital chapel to pray. As she walked in, she spotted two *My Daily Bread* devotional books on the podium, the only two! She thought one for me and one for Mama.

As Joyce sat in the pew, the tears began to flow, and the longer she sat the harder they fell. She looked up at a beautiful statue of Jesus on the cross and began to talk to Him with all her heart. She told Jesus, "I know no one ever suffered like you but please if this is Mama's time, don't let her suffer anymore. Please show us what is wrong and please take away her pain."

The Lord led Joyce to open that devotional book to that particular day; the devotion was called "In the ICU," and the

Scripture reading was, "Yea, though I walk through the valley of the shadow of death, I shall fear no evil." At the bottom of the page were the lyrics to one of Mama's favorite hymns: "It Is Well With My Soul."

Joyce's heart sank further, yet she felt a flutter of peace and knew God had our mother in His arms and, while she did not want Him to take her yet, Mama was ready if He was calling her home.

A lady came into the chapel and recognized Joyce, and Joyce recognized her as Jenny, Mama's physical therapist after she'd had her heart attack. She remembered Joyce being a singer. Joyce shared with her about Mama and, out of the blue, Jenny asked Joyce to sing for her. At first, Joyce thought, *Are you kidding me? I am in here bawling my eyes out, praying and praising God and fussing at Him, and you want me to sing for you?* This was a human moment of a grieving daughter. But Jenny wanted to hear "Surely the Presence" and "Holy Ground." After a few moments Joyce began to sing, and she felt a great sense of peace come over her. As she sang, they both cried. God's presence was all over the chapel ... He was there.

Simultaneously, Debbie held vigil at Mama's side, and Bonnie was in Mama's home praying with healing Scriptures and believing God would once more give us a miracle healing. As Bonnie lay on Mama's home hospital bed, a peace came over her that Mama would be healed. She heard audibly, "Fear not, your mother is not dead but sleeps only!" At the time she thought this meant Mama would be healed and stay here on earth, but she later realized that the message was far greater than her grieving earthly mind was able to conceive at the time. God was telling her that our mother was not dead because her soul would live on, but her life here was over. It would not be the miracle of a physical healing this time, but the greatest miracle healing of all. The only way for Mama to be out of pain at this point was for God to open the gates of heaven for her soul to enter. Her final and most miraculous healing awaited her now. The time was coming to let Mama go.

Mama's shoulder began swelling, and so did her abdomen. Her speech became increasingly slurred and unintelligible. She went from suffering to pure agony. There are no words to describe how your heart feels when you are watching a loved one go through this. Those who have been there can attest to that.

Mama was hurting so badly that she could not stand to be touched anywhere. When she did sleep, she slept hard. When she was awake, it was horrible for her. Pain medication did not help and each day she worsened. They decided to x-ray her shoulder and go in to pull out fluid to relieve the pressure and pain but, unfortunately, there was very little fluid, and it showed no sign of infection.

Even our guardian angel nurse felt defeated. We were blessed to have her with us Monday, Tuesday, and Wednesday. Shanika was not scheduled to be in ICU that week, but God had placed her there for Mama and for us.

Mama was our best friend. She was our every day. We had a very deep connection with her. She had met previous medical challenges, but she always came home.

Mama's kidneys actually began to improve greatly, and her vitals were all normal, with no fever. However, another doctor was called in to assess her. He spoke to us briefly and then began pushing hard on Mama's shoulder and arm. She woke up hollering, and that was upsetting. We told him she was hurting all over, even on pain meds. He flipped our mother on her side which increased her painful moaning. Had he not even bothered to read her chart? Sadly, our mother still could not talk all she could do was cry out in pain. What in the world was happening to Mama? Why would she lose her ability to speak? In this whirlwind of chaos, it seemed sanity walked out the door.

Suddenly, this doctor without any thought or compassion blurted out, "Call in the family and end treatment!" We could hardly believe what we were hearing. How uncaring to just blurt this out to family, and in front of our mother no less! We were hurt by his lack of compassion and totally blindsided at hearing this. This had been a nightmare. Maybe he was right, but no one had told us conclusively what Mama even *had,* and now he was telling us she was dying, let her go!

This doctor told us, "Look, she's eighty-seven, she's a diabetic, and she's had two recent hip surgeries!" We were still grasping this reality, having been thrown into this whirlwind in a short period of time. His obvious conclusion was that we should just consider her life over. YES, she was eighty-seven, but she was a very active eighty-seven with a great mind and love for life. YES, she was a diabetic, but she took good care of herself. And YES, she'd had two hip surgeries, but she had overcome both surgeries, and even with the complications she had, she was doing great. And her kidneys were no longer failing; her vitals were normal and older people do survive bacterial infections.

What he saw was a sick, elderly lady. What *we* saw was a fighter and our mother! OUR MOTHER, not a medical record or number! If she was dying, then at least take us into the hallway and explain things to us, but do not do this in front of her! While she couldn't speak any longer, she could still hear and understand things. What did our sweet mother hear and think? How could he?

The doctor also asked us, if she survived, were we ready for a 24/7 marathon? Sir, if God allowed our mother to live, we would be there for a 24/7 marathon!

We began to call in family and friends as the shock of this turn engulfed us. Then Mama's doctor of twenty years came in, and we shared what the other doctor had just told us and looking shocked she stated, "What?" Then she declared she was not ready to give up on Mama. The antibiotics were working, and Mama's white blood count was coming down. She felt we needed to give it two more days. Once again, the ICU swing was swinging up to the sky, and we agreed, provided Mama would be given pain medicine around the clock. She was not to be in pain anymore.

However, shortly after our meeting with Mama's doctor, we noticed Mama's legs and feet turning cripplingly inward toward the right and drawn into a fetal position. She could no longer move her legs, torso or left arm. It was then that we knew our mother would never walk again … and it was then that we knew she would not want to live like this. The ICU swing came back down hard, but we would follow through on the two more days as all this was sinking in. We knew God had worked miracles for Mama before and He could do it again.

Our brother was beside himself during this week. It was so bittersweet to see him kiss Mama's forehead and tell her he loved her. Her granddaughter, Brittany, was with her holding her hand with tears streaming down her face. She told us that her Maw Maw had opened her eyes and looked up at her shaking her head in a defiant NO! She did not want Brittany to be sad.

A beautiful scene etched in our memories was when Mama's pastor visited her. Mama lay the way her body had collapsed, facing the opposite side of the bed where Pastor Charles stood. As he began to speak, she clearly recognized his voice, and it gave her the strength to turn her head towards him. Her eyes opened wide as he prayed over her and she seemed to find great peace with his presence and his prayer. As he prayed, he gently held her head in his hands, his words to our Lord flowing like music. We watched as he lay her head back on the pillow and she seemed at peace with her soul.

Later that day, Joyce asked Mama if she wanted to fight anymore and Mama shook her head no. We knew Mama was in a place of acceptance and Jesus was near.

On Wednesday evening, Mama's regular doctor came to ICU. The two days she had wanted us to wait had passed. She said everything on paper regarding Mama's health was great, but somehow she was affected by something neurologically and would probably never speak again, she would have mental issues and, no doubt, she would never walk again. Her doctor was baffled. She had picked up her chart on the outside of the hospital room, expecting to walk in and see someone who was very sick, but improving, and someone she could communicate with, but what she saw was something else instead.

With this said, all of our hope was gone. We began a different phase of hurt now ... that of preparing for the letting go of our precious mother.

We felt so guilty. We already had "what if" and "how could this be?" running through our minds. Grief was already creeping in. A four-month battle which, two weeks earlier, we'd thought was won, had reversed course quickly and horrendously destroyed Mama's body, even stealing her ability to speak. It took us all by surprise and suddenly here we were. Mama was not going to go home this time. Home for her now was going to heaven!

Mama was moved from ICU to a comfort care room in hospice. Later that night she was put on a morphine drip. Terminal congestion was beginning. We were with her as she was rolled out of her ICU room and taken to a comfort care room to finish the last leg of her race here on this earth.

After so much pain and crying, when Mama was moved out of ICU, she actually became peaceful. But it did not take away from the fact that we were going to say goodbye to our wonderful mother. The shock was still so fresh. It had happened within such a short period of time.

This experience reminded us of how fast life can change. We were also reminded, as we had been when she had her spinal cord surgery, that as resilient as the body can be, it can be equally as fragile when compromised.

A few years earlier, Mama had given Bonnie a sealed envelope with her last wishes to keep until the time came to open it. That night at the hospital, we gathered in the waiting room and decided to open the envelope, initially thinking it would tell us how she would like her service to be carried out. But Mama had included hand written special messages to us along with two sealed envelopes: one to be opened and read to her children by Mary Barrow at her eulogy, and one to be read at our first Christmas without her. How bittersweet it all was. How heart-wrenching to know it was time. Reading the first line of her message, "I want my children to know they were my reason for living," will resonate in our hearts forever.

Mama was the calmest she had been all week. She was at peace. We don't know what she knew, what she could hear or what she was thinking. There was just a billowing softness about the room. We played beautiful music and kept the room in its stillness. It almost seemed we were the only ones in the entire hospital. Other than the beautiful music, there was no noise.

Mama's best friend, Mary, wanted to come see her, along with Mary's daughter, Wanda and best friend, Regina. These ladies were the hardworking volunteers who were teamed with Mama. They would be the ones to keep the programs going at the VA Hospital. Mary and Wanda lived two hours away, and it was approaching midnight, but they were determined to come and be with Mama.

They arrived around 2:00 a.m. and sat around Mama talking to her quietly. So much love in one room, it could have filled the earth. Oh, how Mama loved these three ladies! They always brightened her day. If only she could have sat up one last time and had a chat, laughed with them and smiled that glow of happiness upon seeing her friends. But she lay very still, and we pray that she heard them talking to her. Mama had always been a part of the conversation, but now all she could do was listen.

When it was time for them to leave, each took her turn not saying goodbye but simply ending with, "We will see you later, and we love you."

Mary leaned in and softly shared these words. "Margaret, as long as I have breath in me, I will continue our work at the VA Hospital. I love you!"

It was now about 4:30 a.m. and time to just lay our heads close to Mama and rest with her.

Thursday morning we were to meet with the hospice staff that would be assisting us in making Mama's journey home a peaceful one. Many friends and family came to visit. We hope she knew they were there.

One visit that stands out was when Diane Rainey came to see Mama. She began to cry very hard as she sat beside her and held her hand. Diane loved Mama, and Mama loved Diane. Diane always said that when Mama brought a program to the patients, she knew she never had to worry about anything because "Mrs. Glenn always knew what she wanted and did it right." We don't know who was sobbing more at that moment, Diane or us. We were all deeply touched to witness how much she loved our mother. We so hope Mama felt her love.

During this visit, the chaplain from the hospital dropped by to check on us, and Diane asked if she could speak to him privately. Her faith was being challenged because Mama had suffered so greatly when she had been such a good person and a faithful servant of the Lord. She needed some words of comfort from the chaplain so she could find peace with this and to help her understand. How wonderful is God's perfect timing to have the chaplain come by at just the right moment. He came by to comfort us but, instead, God had sent him to comfort one of God's hurting children ... Diane.

The season of death certainly brings with it a new perspective on how we look at the things of this life, and we quickly find out what is important and what is not. The journey we take in this life can have real purpose, and the legacy we leave after our journey here on earth has the potential to continue impacting others for generations. Why the suffering? We will never fully understand while we are here; but we have to rely on our faith and know that once that threshold is passed over into heaven, all is well with our souls.

*...As were all our fathers our days on
the earth are as a shadow ...*
1 Chronicles 29:15 KJV

Those four special ladies sharing final moments with Mama brought beautiful warmth that only soul-friendship can bring. As we watched them with Mama and watched them leave, we began to realize that everyone's journey truly does matter. Within every season of life, each one of us can create enormous synergy and bonds that cannot be broken, relationships that will live on here and in heaven.

Mama's body began to hurt again, and the levels of morphine were increased. Meds were given to help with the terminal congestion. Her labored breathing and moaning were very upsetting, but this was the process. They finally removed the oxygen from her nose, as she kept pushing it off with her right hand again. We know with her doing this, she was still aware and simply did not want it.

Family members took turns holding her hand and just being beside her, reconciling in their hearts that it was time to say goodbye to their much loved Maw Maw: a mother, a grandmother, a great-grandmother and a mother-in-law.

Thursday night we decided to dim the lights as we gathered around her. Debbie, who had diligently kept the hospital vigil, stayed close at hand by Mama. Bonnie had been at the foot of her bed all day, loving and massaging her precious legs and feet, remembering their quest for shoes. Joyce took a wedged pillow and leaned into it from a chair so she could sit at Mama's right side and hold her hand. We prayed over her and loved on her. We played her favorite songs softly, in hopes she could hear them. We dozed off and on that night. At times it seemed Mama was just sleeping, not dying.

The sun rose again on Friday morning, and Mama was still with us. When her doctor came by while making rounds, we had a heart-wrenching conversation with her about disabling Mama's pacemaker to allow Mama to pass away naturally. It just seemed wrong to let her lie here, lingering for possibly a few more days or even weeks, on a morphine drip. Mama would not have wanted that. Her doctor agreed and honestly felt it would be best. We knew this was the right thing to do so we could allow Mama to take her last trip, "just a little ways down the road."

About 1:00 p.m., a tech came into the room with the equipment to disable Mama's pacemaker. It startled us at first, as we thought we were prepared, but the reality of what was about to take place overwhelmed us, and we fell apart. Our reaction apparently scared this young man, and he calmly left the room. Soon a nurse came in and took Joyce out in the hallway to ask her if we still wanted to do this. She said we needed to be ready because it was going to shorten Mama's time. Joyce responded that this was such a hard decision to make, but it was the right thing to do.

About 3:00 p.m., the technician returned to the room to disengage Mama's pacemaker. Her race was moments from being over.

What we didn't expect was what happened next.

CHAPTER 9

The Gift

*Oh Lord my God, I called to you for
help and you healed me.*
Psalm 30:2 NIV

It's 3:00 p.m., Friday, May 3, 2013. Life goes on outside these hospital walls. But in Room 6009, the beating of our mother's beautiful heart is about to cease.

The radiant spring sun shone through the window, cascading beams of light throughout the room and creating a most peaceful atmosphere, as Mama drew closer to entering a light even more brilliant to meet Jesus face-to-face.

It had been an arduous two weeks. Fatigued and weary, we had stayed the course. Our brother Lockwood had returned home brokenhearted. Deep down he felt the need to spend time with Mama's precious dog, Little Moe, fulfilling his promise to always take care of him.

As we looked upon our mother, it seemed so unfair to allow her to continue in this state of limbo any longer with organs failing and constant terminal congestion. Friday morning with heavy broken hearts, a discussion was had with Mama's doctor to disable her pacemaker so she could pass naturally.

When Mama's pacemaker was disabled, we were shocked when her body reacted as though she had been revived with heart paddles rather than moving into a deeper restful state. At first, we regretted the decision. She had been slumbering in a beautiful place of peacefulness, and the jolt had disturbed and startled her. But this would prove to be a blessed decision which opened a spiritual door to a gift from God through our mother that we will forever remember and share.

They say our eyes are the windows to our soul. Our mama opened her eyes for the first time in three days and began looking around. Her eyes were like glass and almost twinkling with a radiant pale blue hue with a brilliant aura. Mama should have been blind, yet she seemed to have vision as she looked at each one of us and about the room. Unable to move her head, she used only her eyes to look around.

"Hey Mama," Joyce said, sitting to Mama's right and holding her hand.

"We love you, Mama," Bonnie said from the foot of her bed where she held her vigil.

"Love you, Mama," Debbie cried as she caressed Mama's left shoulder.

"We love you, and we will miss you," we all said in unison as tears flowed.

All this interaction was bringing her too far back into our world, so we decided to speak very calmly and softly to her. Heartbroken, we agreed that we shouldn't talk to her much at all, as she needed to continue her transition in peace. It was all so mind-numbingly surreal.

As the room became quiet, she once again grew relaxed, and within moments she closed her eyes and fell back into a transitioning slumber. The room filled with a sense of serenity.

There was only the soft whirring sound of the air conditioner as we each kept our place of vigil around our mama.

Our last forty minutes with Mama held events we could never have imagined. The family and friends who were still at the hospital had gathered in the waiting area. Knowing her time was short, we remained around Mama's bed.

A prayer warrior from the church where Mama was a member, Tammy Adams, came by to visit. She prayed the most spiritually eloquent prayer over Mama and prayed for us as well. We once again began talking to Mama in very soft tones while she made her transition. As comforting as it was that she was going to heaven, it was the saddest and heaviest our hearts have ever felt.

There was now a presence in this room creating an atmosphere of stillness, setting the pace for what God had prepared for us. *For what was about to happen was the most divine scene we could have ever imagined.*

Mama opened her radiant blue eyes again and looked at Joyce. There was such peace in her eyes, and she clearly had vision as she locked eyes with her youngest daughter. While still holding Mama's hand, Joyce told her softly to go to the arms of Jesus. Then Mama looked at Bonnie at the foot of the bed. With tears flowing, Bonnie could only nod her head in agreement with Joyce, letting Mama know she was saying goodbye, and it was time to go to the arms of Jesus.

Mama, blind in the physical, locked her "soul eyes" on Bonnie. Suddenly Bonnie, with much surprise in her voice, said, "Oh my gosh ... she's moving her feet." Sobbing now, Bonnie continued repeating, "She's moving her feet...her feet and her legs are moving!"

As her feet moved closer to Bonnie, Mama's right foot pushed through the sheet and pressed against her leg. A few seconds later Mama's left foot pushed through the sheet and pressed against Bonnie's hip! The energy from her soul was emerging from her dying physical shell with strength and power beyond anything of this world.

With tears in her eyes, Bonnie said, "They are so strong! So powerful! They are healed!" Mama's crippled, paralyzed, disjointed legs which had been drawn into a fetal position were now healed and made whole. Mama wanted Bonnie to know she wouldn't be needing those shoes after all.

Mama had not and could not move her legs, and yet we were experiencing this phenomenal event. Joyce began to tell Mama to **run** into the arms of Jesus. **"Don't walk Mama, RUN!"**

We watched as Mama looked up towards the corner of the room. Mama could not speak, but her eyes said it all. Who was there? She wanted to go with whoever had come to show her the way.

Joyce, still holding Mama's right hand tightly in both of her hands felt a pull.

Suddenly, with great force, Mama pulled her hand away from Joyce's tight grip. She lifted her right arm with strength into the air to take someone's hand. And then slowly, gracefully and in complete control, her right arm beautifully and amazingly began a deliberate descent. Her arm rested gently upon her chest with her hand over her heart, her eyes closed, her last breath taken, Mama was gone.

Joyce asked, "Did you see that?"

"Yes!" Bonnie replied. "Yes, YES I did."

Mama's arm did not just drop down on her body as one might expect; it gracefully came down in a beautifully orchestrated manner. As we pondered this, we realized it was a sign to Debbie, who was at Mama's left side. She was waving goodbye to her. It was breathtaking to behold. Her arm, in slow motion, cascaded across her chest after letting go. It was such a peaceful, soft-focus moment.

It was a heavenly scene of wonder as the portal to heaven had opened and someone was there to take Mama's hand. Everything we had experienced in those last minutes was a blessed gift from God. Our mother had been healed before our very eyes, and Jesus had allowed us to experience her seeing us and feeling her soul leave her body … with her legs and feet strong. By pulling her hand away from Joyce, we knew she was letting go and going to her eternal home! We were in awe!

Mama's race ended with a final burst of healing. Truly, she ran into the arms of Jesus. Astonishingly, in those last moments, there was no struggle to breathe, no anxiety, no pain, no clinching, no gurgling, no fear, no indication of suffering at all. It was evident Mama was filled with the fullness of grace. Through the death of her body, her soul was released to enter the gates of heaven, her eternal home. She was awake, aware and we witnessed her vividly transcending to Glory. For whatever reasons, God allowed her to tell us in the only way she could that she was healed, that she was leaving and that she was ready. It was a most exquisite exit, and a gift we will cherish forever.

We knew what Mama was saying to us when she pulled her hand away from Joyce. "It's time to let me go, children. Know that I am okay and I am ready to go home to be with the Lord. I am healed and in no more pain. My legs and feet are strong, and I can run Miss me, but let me go."

Oh, how it did our hearts good to know Mama was walking and running without pain, just as she had as a young girl! Those strong, athletic legs of her youth were once again a part of her.

We had all prayed so much for healing and our will when, ultimately, it was God's will to be done. Our mother was now with Jesus. As hard as those last eight days were for her, what a blessing and a privilege to have been with her even through the agony, but especially in her final moments to see God's amazing, saving grace receive and heal our precious mother instantly.

*Jesus conquered death on the cross ...
and He conquered the grave through His resurrection.*

---

*That Christ may dwell in your hearts through faith;
that you, being rooted and grounded in love,
may be able to comprehend with all the saints what
is the width and length and depth and height—
to know the love of Christ which passes knowledge;
that you may be filled with all the fullness of God.*
Ephesians 3:17-19 NKJV

Our Reason ... Our Purpose

We believe God wants us to share this powerful unveiling of eternal life and the seasons of life through our mother's journey ... her life, her struggles, her faith and, in the end, even her suffering ... so that it may help others in some way. While God expects us to plant the seeds of the promise of heaven, it is ultimately He to whom we give all the glory and praise.

There are times when healing can only come when we leave this physical body. Mama's final healing miracle was complete. She would never need a miracle again. The reality of Jesus having conquered death and the grave is more real to us now than ever before.

We believe Mama left her footprints for us to always remember that those legs and feet were permanently healed. Bonnie felt the impression on her hip where Mama had pushed into her with great strength, until Sunday night, when the sensation began to fade. She fondly refers to those impressions as footprints from Mama. While pulling her hand away from Joyce's and her arm cascading so beautifully towards Debbie, we know it was her letting us go.

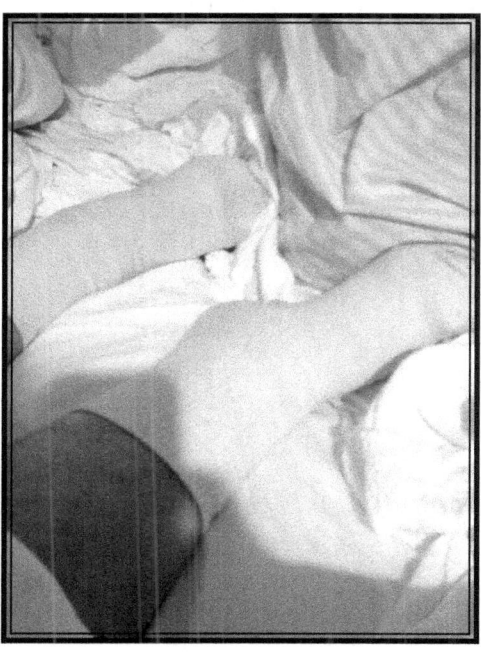

Mama's sweet feet pressing against Bonnie. She had been crippled, and in a fetal position but in the end, she could move her legs and feet ... in her weakness He made her strong!

For those who may doubt that God and heaven exist, please know: They do! The soul does indeed leave the body and live on in a different time and place. No more physical pain. No more struggles.

Mama had run a good race. It was time now for this race to end and a new and far better one to begin. And this new one would be forever in a body that could not know disease or pain or sorrow or hardships. Oh, how she must have felt like a child again with complete energy and life!

Almost immediately after Mama left us, she looked like herself again. The agony of whatever had destroyed her body was gone. Remember the photograph Joyce took of Mama and deleted? Mama had not looked like herself since that Saturday. Mama was a beautiful lady but whatever took control of her body and destroyed it, also stole her beauty. But in the end, her beauty was restored.

I will restore health unto thee, and I will heal thee of thy wounds, saith the LORD...
Jeremiah 30:17 KJV

I have fought a good fight, I have finished my course, I have kept the faith: henceforth there is laid up for me a crown of righteousness, which the Lord, the righteous judge, shall give me at that day: and not to me only, but unto all them also that love his appearing.
2 Timothy 4:7–8 KJV

Yes, to love with all your heart and soul is to experience great joy, but it is also to experience equally profound sorrow at the loss of one who was loved so greatly. But we believe it is so worth it.

The seasons of life come and go. As the ebb of the tide's cyclic flow, many of the mysteries of life still lie in the unknown. It is a quest to find our purpose in life, or rather to question and seek the answers: What is life without purpose? Where do we go from here? We have life, and then we pass from this life to eternal life. Or do we simply have nothing? What do you believe?

Precious in the sight of the Lord is the death of his saints.
Psalm 116:15 KJV

PART 4

From Grief to Healing

A time to rend, and a time to sew, a time to keep silence, and a time to speak; A time to love, and a time to hate; a time of war, and time of peace.
Ecclesiastes 3:7-8 KJV

CHAPTER  10

Entering the Valley of Grief

*For he is not a God of the dead but of
the living: for all live unto him.*
Luke 20:38 KJV

*A note to you from our family: The months following
December 22, 2012, during which we cared for our
mother, were challenging and exhausting, yet a time full
of heartfelt dedication to our mother who had always
been there for us. May God bless all those who have or
are lovingly caring for a loved one. It is a journey well
worth every second, no matter how intense. For when
those days are over ... you will wish you had done more.*

The room is quiet after Mama's passing as we give ourselves a moment to embrace this new world. Word is sent to the waiting room, where other family members were gathered sharing wonderful "Maw Maw" stories with tears, love, warmth and laughter. As they enter her room, that love and warmth fill the air as each one gives a kiss, a hug, and a "love you and will miss you" to Mama. As our hearts are reeling from the finality of this, the hospital staff encourages us to take all the time we need. Then the time comes for us to take our first step of life without Mama and we walk out of Room 6009, never to return.

It is final. Our numbness remains intact as emotions come into play. We must accept that Mama is not coming home with us this time. Although Mama's feet are with Jesus now, our feet begin to feel the heaviness of weights with each step as we walk away from her and out of the hospital.

Soon we arrive at Mama's home and enter her front door. The reality hit hard that our lives are forever changed. It is a most gut-wrenching feeling. We feel enshrined in a thick fog, an odd fog we will experience on numerous occasions to come. Seeing and touching her personal belongings, medications, Bible and study notes exactly where everything was left, never to be used again, well, it is just breathtakingly sad. Our hearts and souls are weeping, but there is no time to stop and grieve completely. There is much that needs to be done in a short period of time.

There was shopping to do for a beautiful gown for Mama, and we had to contact the people we needed for hair and makeup. We wanted to be sure she looked beautiful! Who better to do this than Mama's own hairdresser and two wonderful makeup artists, close friends, Janie, Sharon, and Glenda? Our hearts grieved, our breath sometimes stalled, our minds struggled with all that had to be done.

In grief, oftentimes, you do not think rationally. While shopping, we wanted Mama to have a beautiful nightgown and lingerie. In our craziness, we happened upon this beautiful pink bra with a sparkling rhinestone, and it just talked to us. Mama had to have this. We knew she would think this was so pretty and she would have loved the sparkling rhinestone as it would shine so beautifully through her lovely pink gown! As we made our way to the register, we found quickly what she would not have been thrilled with ... the bra rang up as $60.00!! We had not looked at the price tag but, you know what, it did not matter. Mama probably had never spent much over $60.00 on bras in her entire life. Yes, it was a moment of indulgence and was well worth it, but, in the end, the rhinestone didn't even show through the gown. The funeral director, bless his heart, tried so hard to make this happen but it just did not work. That was okay, though, as we knew Mama still would have loved the bra and we knew the rhinestone was there. Maybe we were crazy, but this comes with the rollercoaster ride of the grief cycle. Mama looked beautiful and peaceful, and that is all that mattered.

As we juggled all these details with mindless wonder, it was time to revisit Mama's last wishes and plan her Celebration of Life service. She had it all written out exactly as she wanted and the next few days were spent preparing for Tuesday, May 7, 2013. A lengthy list to be completed, we were grateful for Mama's precious last wishes and messages, without which we were not sure we could have pulled it off! Only a few alterations had to be made, so for the most part, we were able to plan her finale as she wished. It was a most beautiful tribute, one she would have applauded and one where the Lord was truly glorified.

Her service was signature Mama! Her Pastor delivered a meaningful message and the exquisite voices of those she had chosen to sing filled our hearts with the glory of God. One of her grandsons, Brandon, decided he would like to share some "Maw Maw" moments and as emotional as it was, Joyce's heart was determined to fulfill Mama's request to sing Babbie Mason's "All Rise."

The program was arrayed with Mama's selected Scriptures and poems. Mary Barrow read the poem Mama had left in a sealed envelope to be read to her children at her eulogy. The poem had a handwritten message on it that said, "Read to my children" and another little note that read "Say something good about me! Ha-Ha! Love all of you." The poem, author unknown, was entitled:

MISS ME BUT LET ME GO

When I come to the end of the road
And the sun has set for me
I want no rites in a gloom-filled room.
Why cry for a soul set free?

Miss me a little – but not too long
And not with your head bowed low.
Remember the love that we once shared,
Miss me – but let me go.

For this is a journey that we all must take
And each must go alone.

It's all a part of the Master's plan,
A step on the road to home.
When you are lonely and sick of heart
Go to the friends we know
And bury your sorrows in doing good deeds.
Miss Me – But Let me Go!

We did not know what Mary would be reading until she stood before us and opened the envelope. It was so Mama! This poem had so much relevance with how Mama let us go in those last few moments. And then Mary did indeed say some good things about her. It was joyous as Mama would have wanted. We were so in awe of the little messages she left for us to read after she was gone. How thoughtful it was to leave just that precious little bit more of her here with us! While we held tight to "the gift" given to us during Mama's passing, we would not escape the depths of grief. As the dust continued to settle, more tasks needed immediate attention. Each new phase required baby steps, as it seemed there was a new task at hand at every turn. One of the most heartbreaking moments was calling to have Mama's hospital bed removed. We each took turns lying in it, feeling Mama one last time. When the company arrived to remove it, well, that feeling cannot be described. Trembling, we watched it being dismantled and taken out to the van; we turned and stood in her bedroom door, staring at the empty space, with pain so intense it took our breath away. Some thought we should be filled with joy that she no longer needed a sick bed; yet for us, our hearts were not in tune to that joy, rather it received a jolt of reality. We were going to miss our mother terribly. This void was going to be huge, and we knew it.

It hurt. Grief was no longer knocking at the door; it had entered, and it had entered with great force.

Questions would abound and haunt us as to what exactly had happened to Mama and how this curtain closed so rapidly. Flashbacks to those days in ICU were unbearable. We learned quickly that this was going to be a process, and not an easy one. We were being led into a valley we had never trodden before. Each day brought something new with it.

One of our saddest days came as we began packing up and cleaning out her home. Driving into her driveway to begin this process sent shock waves through us. Tears flowed as we laid eyes on the handicap ramp built just four months earlier by her sons-in-law, Larry and Tony. Our eyes followed the ramp to the door—the door to enter the house, as we had done so many times over the years, knowing Mama was there. The door that allowed us to enter our mama's world was no longer and our new reality continued to greet us head-on. Memories flooded through and emptiness ensued in the pit of our stomachs like nothing we'd ever felt before. We did not like this season! Initially, the house felt empty and, yet, you could feel the presence of Mama's love and life filling every room. Oh, how we missed her, her voice, her laughter, her spirit. "Oh Lord, how we miss her!"

Blessed are those who mourn, for they shall be comforted.
Matthew 5:4, NKJV

Grief wasn't new to us. We grieved the loss of our father in 1970 and the loss of many relatives and close friends over the years. So we knew the toll grief could extract from one's heart and mind. But this was different. It was deeper, and unlike any grief we had ever experienced. It was more painful, more intense. This was our mother. She was the matriarch of our family and the one with whom we'd had the deepest bond. We knew she was in heaven. We never doubted her destiny. That was evident in her faith and the gift given to us as she went to heaven. But, when in the throes of deep sorrow, that knowledge didn't always ease our pain. A piece of our family puzzle was missing. The life that had once filled the rooms of this house was now in the past, leaving us with memories to hold tightly. Our minds relentlessly walked through every remembrance of her life within this house, nestling each memory within our hearts. We were indeed naïve, as we had never seen ourselves living our lives without our mama.

It didn't take long to learn how dark, torturous and complex this valley could be. So many different emotions take on lives of their own. The pressure of anger, guilt, sadness, unanswered questions and other emotions can become overwhelming. Possibly her illness could have been prevented. Had her unexpected decline happened because of something we did or didn't do? And yet here we are! All this anxiety created a vacuum that, at times, seemed inescapable. Now we had to learn to live our lives with broken hearts that kept on beating, giving us life. Somehow it felt deceitful and unfair. The master of deceit was clawing at us, causing us to feel we had failed our mother.

Mama left this earth at 3:40 p.m. on Friday, May 3, 2013. Her final cause of death was listed as "sepsis." The cycle of questions continuously haunted us: Where did this bacterial infection come from? When and why did it go septic? Why were there no tests up front for this deadly disease, particularly for a high-risk patient? Why don't doctors pay more attention to the symptoms of sepsis or bacterial infections? We recognize God's mercy in taking our mother in the end, but these questions lay heavy upon our hearts.

Come unto me, all ye that labour and are heavy laden, and I will give you rest. Take my yoke upon you, and learn of me; for I am meek and lowly in heart; and ye shall find rest unto your souls. For my yoke is easy, and my burden is light.
Matthew 11:28–30 KJV

There were times when our hearts felt so broken, seemingly resistant to the healing process. Every tear that fell was filled with intense pain. Mama was gone! That thought cut so deeply to the core of our being. There were those who said, "She was eighty-seven; she lived a long life." Implying we should just get over this already. Yes, this was true, but *she was our mother; these were our hearts that were hurting* and, as she had grown older, our bond with her had become even greater. We deserved some time to get used to this huge void and this new season of our lives.

Grief is a human and spiritual journey, and it yields with it difficulties that take time to process. The human aspects encompassed those gnawing questions, which continued still to somehow have life. We sought answers daily. We retrieved her medical records. We questioned God. We bitterly thought that we had done everything we were supposed to do: believe, trust, and stand with great faith in the healing power of Jesus. And it hadn't worked. Yes, even as Christians, we found ourselves drowning in a pool of confusion and gut-wrenching pain. We desperately grasped for understanding of how and why everything had unfolded as it did. We so desperately needed this settled in our hearts and minds. We needed to find peace and make peace with ourselves that we had done everything we could. It wasn't our fault. The spiritual aspect is seeking, finding and settling into that place of peace and letting go of the human aspects.

But they that wait upon the LORD shall renew their strength; they shall mount up with wings as eagles; they shall run and not be weary, and they shall walk, and not faint.
Isaiah 40:31 KJV

As for God, his way is perfect: the word of the LORD is tried: he is a buckler to all those that trust him.
Psalm 18:30 KJV

In the immediate aftermath of losing Mama, there were short spurts of numbness within. It was akin to walking through life but not being totally present. Life huddled in a deep fog, with the body present but the surroundings distant. Perhaps this is a mechanism God put in place to help us through. Maybe, in some strange way, it preserves our sanity during these times.

Grief brings with it many challenges, but we are realizing this can be a journey of great discovery as well. No one is okay with losing a loved one. The void is too great. It hurts. No loss is the same. God knows our pain. In our minds, we knew He was always just, always right, but allowing His truth to flourish in our hearts was challenging at times. In the times when it seemed hopeless to recover, we began to realize we were stronger than we thought. As long as we could get up every morning and breathe, we were strong enough to get through another day.

The anger within our grief was, at times, relentless. Often, we were angry with ourselves, angry with God, angry with each other, angry with doctors and even angry with someone else, anyone else. But probably the biggest stronghold of our grief was guilt. Guilt can consume you and eat you from the inside out if not kept in check. Certain scenes and scenarios just want to play over and over again in your mind, making you wish you had done this or that. What if? What if? What if? If only. If only. If only.

But nothing can change the past. You don't get a do-over. Yet this particular play harnesses your mind and repeats itself over and over again as though somehow, someway, if it plays enough times, it will bring in the desired outcome. The harsh truth must be accepted: we can never go back and start over. We ponder all the questions we will never have conclusive answers for. The desire for everything to be resolved in our minds has to be denied, and that defies all nature. Struggling, we must accept that we are where we are, and we must deal in the now. Nothing can change it. We must change!

He heals the broken hearted and binds up their wounds.
Psalm 147:3 KJV

Treading this valley requires a tremendous balancing act dealing with the full array of sadness, anger, guilt, feeling stuck in limbo, the heaviness of your feet with each step that makes you feel as though you are dragging thousand-pound weights behind you … the breathlessness.

Then there are those times you feel paralyzed, unable to think, feel or move at all, as well as the sudden flow of tears when you least expect them. Getting through all this can be like plowing a field with a mule and, every time you look back, it has to be plowed all over again. It's demanding, and it's exhausting, but that is what makes you determined to get through this valley to the other side where there are light and peace, where the roller coaster ride ends.

The Lord is my strength and my shield; my heart trusted in him, and I am helped: therefore my heart greatly rejoiceth; and with my song will I praise him.
Psalm 28:7 KJV

The time came to start going through Mama's personal belongings and papers and to begin the process of letting go. And we found we were not very good at it! We had avoided this as long as we could. It is so hard to let go of someone's life, but we could not continue holding on to things that needed to go, like old checkbooks and bank statements and so many other things of this nature. Going through these things, we would see her handwriting, her notations, her thoughts, her signature, her work and her life in every little detail on so many seemingly insignificant things. And our dear Mama held on to a lot of papers and statements, some going back twenty and thirty years!

Her monthly medicine compartment container still filled with medications, pills she never came home to take, was bittersweet. Holding the zipper pouch with her diabetic needles and blood sugar calculator and the insulin pen, knowing it would never be used again, brought tears. Oh yes, we rejoiced that she was forever off these medications and insulin and, goodness, having to prick those fingers. But it sure was hard to look at those things she never came home to use again. We held on to Mama's white Christmas tree, but when it was pulled out to put up that first Christmas without her, we discovered it had turned brown. It seemed to have mourned her passing and didn't want to be used anymore.

It is all the little things that are the hardest to deal with because there are so many of them. And while they may have seemed insignificant in the past, they are now filled with meaning beyond description. For now, the purse Mama was using, her wallet, her debit card, the little candies in the bottom of that purse in case of a sugar drop, and the little gift bag she always carried to the beauty parlor with her twenty-six bobby pins and hairpiece, will all have a home with us for a while longer. As time goes on another release is in our future, perhaps two or more, but who's counting?

As all those little tangible traces of a person's life are slowly but surely let go, they seem to scream at you, proclaiming, "Yes, she was here, but now she is gone. Let her go." It is excruciatingly sad to erase another's life in bits and pieces. But in the right time, we will continue to set these things free. With every season of releasing, we tuck the past away safely in our hearts. We make exceptions for pictures, videos, voice recordings and precious little remnants that are of value to us. For those articles of clothing and garments we can't dare part with, we will have memory quilts made so we will always have a little bit of Mama to cuddle up with. The memories of all our years with Mama flood our hearts daily. It was a long ride—and yet it was short.

CHAPTER

Facing the Firsts

"Grief can challenge our faith, but grief is not the absence of faith but rather the presence of great love."
Bonnie Jennings

For those of you who have lost loved ones, you know how challenging facing 'the firsts' can be. But the truth is, these firsts prove to be part of the grief healing process. It was just two weeks after Mama's passing, and we faced our first event without her. It was one of the hardest things we had to do. It was time to attend her four-year-old great-granddaughter's kindergarten graduation, which was being held in the same church where Mama was a member and where we had just had her service. It was the church she insisted on going to the Sunday she was becoming ill. She had always attended the kids' events, and there were many at this church. Mama had been looking forward to attending this graduation, and it was written on her calendar. It was so hard to remain seated when we wanted to run out. It was torturous, to be frank. We endured because we knew Mama would never want to lessen or take anything away from one of these children. Afterward, we went to Krispy Kreme, just as we had done in the past. Again, Mama never would have wanted to take any joy away from Taylor's special event, so we pushed through the pain for Mama and for Taylor. Life goes on!

Our first Mother's Day without her came quickly, followed by the Fourth of July. Then Mama's birthday ... that was a hard one! Soon fall was in the air, with nature's decorations of beautiful gold and orange leaves. This ushered in a welcome cooling down from the hot South Carolina summer. She loved this season. Halloween was bittersweet because she so enjoyed all the festivities and we so missed all the little sweet things she did for the children.

Thanksgiving came upon us, and it was going to be hard to face an empty chair at the table. It was one of those breathless challenges, so we decided not to have our traditional family gathering. Our hearts heavy, some of us gathered at a restaurant for Thanksgiving dinner. Others decided to go out of town for a change of pace. Nothing felt the same. Yet as sad as our hearts were, we gave thanks knowing we were blessed to have had so many Thanksgivings with our mother. This was going to take some getting used to.

Christmas! The most wonderful time of the year ... the first Christmas after you lose a loved one, there is melancholy in the spirit of the season. Grateful for so much, yet our hearts really longed for what used to be. We missed preparing delicious meals for Christmas Day with Mama. We missed the smell of coffee brewing, hot grits, her wonderful fried chicken and biscuits with gravy for Christmas breakfast. We greatly missed her hustling and bustling about to get her Christmas shopping done, her beautiful white and pink Christmas tree, her laughter and her holiday spirit. She always expressed her love for the Lord but especially as she celebrated this special time of year, remembering the gift of salvation given to us by the birth of our Savior, Jesus Christ.

Oh, how our hearts ached at the thought of gathering at Mama's resting place with the sealed envelope she had marked "to be opened the first Christmas after I am gone." It was a beautiful poem, "My First Christmas in Heaven" by —Wanda Bencke.

The poem was read aloud, embraced with Mama's favorite Christmas music in the background. Our hearts tugged for strength as sadness engulfed us with tears. It was one of those dreamlike moments as we stood there as close as we could get to her physical body. We were spending Christmas with Mama ... just in a different way.

The New Year rolled in, then came Easter, and *wham*, the first anniversary of the illness and her passing. With each new first ... baby steps. These things take time.

Time refused to stand still. It moved right on without a blink and without a conscience at all. The sun rose and set as though nothing had happened, and business went on as usual for everyone around us. It was just our lives affected by this. Tears fell, hearts ached, but life had to keep moving. Another new day begins and ends without a care. Our lives moved on in a different world. All around, life for everyone else continued without pause, and it was sometimes hard to see others in their season of happiness. We pondered when that season would return for us, but for now, this was the journey we were on. We wished time would stand still and wait on us to get through this, but that wasn't going to happen. It seemed time was not our friend but, rather, our foe.

Seconds become invaluable segments of time when someone is about to take their last breath. The clock is ticking. Second by second is going by. Every second counts!

The ticking clock stops when earthly life ends, and the soul takes entrance into a timeless heaven.

In our grief cycle, time was counted and measured relentlessly. Time took on a strange significance as we constantly recounted the seconds, minutes, hours, days, weeks and months after Mama's passing. We measured time by the second of the passing, the minute of the passing, the hour of the passing, the day of the passing, the week and the date of the passing. It seemed insane, but it proves to be quite sane as the process of healing continues.

A time to every purpose under heaven…In the beginning, these specific anniversary dates are painful. In the end, time became our ally, a friend in the healing process. It's cliché, but it's true: time is what it takes to heal. It plays a significant role in finding peace. Each second is either lost or effective in the healing process as those anniversary moments of time become precious remnants of a life once among us.

Those horrible, painful moments in the hospital and the initial grip of grief upon losing our mother, the sadness we felt at her Celebration of Life service and burial and the first months that followed were extremely traumatic but, with the passage of time, we have found some easing. We will always miss Mama, and we will always grieve that she is no longer with us. We are still a work in progress. Even so, some healing has found a place. While seeing certain places, photos, or just memories can trigger pain just as excruciating as it was in the beginning, we realize this is a part of the process. Grief is hard; there is just no way around it. And each person's time frame for healing is different.

> *...a time to heal; a time to break down, and a time to build up; A time to weep, and a time to laugh; a time to mourn, and a time to dance;*
> Ecclesiastes 3:3-4 KJV

The darkness within the valley is incredibly powerful, and we quickly discovered that even as faithful followers of Christ, how cruel this season could be. At times the beautiful, comforting Scriptures didn't seem to help and even that created guilt in our hearts. Even so, we intended to rely on those Scriptures, because we knew our quest for that divine, tranquil peace could only come through God.

> *Peace I leave with you, my peace I give unto you: not as the world giveth, give I unto you. Let not your heart be troubled, neither let it be afraid.*
> John 14:27 KJV

> *Grief knows no boundaries; therefore we must create them.*

Grief can be truly agonizing, and Christians are not immune to the pain or sting of losing loved ones. It takes a conscious effort to keep pushing through. Deep within our souls, we held tight to our belief that a new and strengthened faith was waiting to emerge on the other side of this quest for restoration. As Christians, we knew the only way out of the darkness of this valley was to seek the light of Jesus—to journey through grief to that place of tranquility that only Jesus could lead us to. No person on the planet could take us there. No words spoken could lead us there. But when we are in the deepest, darkest part of the valley, it's easy to be temporarily blinded by the darkness.

There are no shortcuts. We have to go through the painful process to get there. We have to tread the valley. We have to ride the seemingly endless roller coaster that exhausts you beyond exhaustion. And there are times you feel pretty darn near dead yourself. At some point, you surely must desire to see where this ride ends so you can finally get off.

When something traumatic blindsides you, you find yourself in the middle of a spiral with all the things you know about God swirling on the outside while the sudden, intense pain of grief engulfs you on the inside, creating a battle of humanity versus spirituality. Spiritually we held on to our belief that there was power behind continuing to praise God during our suffering. In this season of life and grief, we had to learn to connect the human journey with the spiritual journey; the grief journey with the praise journey.

Looking back, we know our prayers and pleas for healing *were* heard, but God answered in a different way than we hoped. He did what was right and just and we are coming to terms with that. God always has the last word and that word certainly is not death, but the greatest gift of life everlasting in His kingdom. We hold tight to the truth that we will one day be with our mother again.

Knowing that life indeed exists beyond this earthly vessel doesn't negate the fact that grief will befriend you. Oh, how you miss the sound of their voice, their very presence, everything that was them. But this is a season of life no one will escape. We will all say our temporary goodbyes to loved ones and we will one day be the loved one being said goodbye to. God promises to send a Comforter in these times, and He promises to show us how to fill that void with something good. This creates the boundaries that help in the healing process of grief. Although in the midst of this storm we often struggle to claim these promises with confidence, there will come a time when we will.

---

*Therefore, if any man be in Christ, he is a
new creature; old things are passed away;
behold, all things are become new.*
2 Corinthians 5:17 KJV

CHAPTER 12

The Passage to Peace

Mama somehow was always able to find pleasure in her life among the thorns. She focused on the rosebuds ... always waiting to bloom. During those times when the thorns were very prickly and painful, the image of that blooming rosebud stayed in clear view of her lens of life.

As we dealt with the intensity of our grief, we began to realize that there was something more being exposed here than just losing our mother. When Mama was here with us, we found much of our strength through her, the woman we saw push through so many obstacles in our childhood and throughout her life. Now our earthly childhood savior was gone. All of our past experiences from childhood flooded into this mixture of grief. Memories of our father, long gone but not forgotten, lay heavy on our minds and we began to realize that Mama was the clasp that held our family together, that held our past together. Our relationship with her had a dynamic that we did not fully understand until she was gone.

We lived it all ... the good, the bad, and the ugly. We had learned to survive and adapt in many situations. Mama never saw herself as a victim, but as a fighter, a survivor. Somehow when she passed away, our grief became entangled with our past. Our chain was broken when her silver cord was loosed.

As we chart our way through this maze of grief, we are seeing that as we moved forward from our childhood, we had brought unresolved grief along with us all our lives. We had unresolved grief not only for the loss of our father but over the relationship we never had with him. We had unresolved grief from many traumatic childhood experiences. It's easier to suppress memories than deal with them, as over time these unpleasantries fade or hide within us, so we don't take the time to make peace with them. We just take them along with us.

It is time now to regroup and adapt to our new reality. To rise above all these mountains is what our mother expects of us and what God expects us to do.

For I the LORD thy God will hold thy right hand,
Saying unto thee, FEAR not: I will help thee.
Isaiah 41:13 KJV

With much reflecting and traveling back to our past in these last two and a half years of writing this book, we realize that as we heal, our perspectives of our past are changing. We understand things better. Healing is allowing those trials, hardships, and pain to gently begin to fade as we make peace with them. We see our father in a way we never did before. As for our mother, we see the raw beauty of the magnificent connection we had with her.

Through this passage into peace, it is a harrowing task to keep the mind in the right place. It seems negativity comes more naturally and easily. The void will always be there. The important thing now is to fill that void with something good and not allow anything negative to take a stronghold. While Mama can never be replaced, the void can be filled with something that reflects the good memories of her life and helps in our healing processes as well as sharing the good news of Jesus Christ. Her journey is now our journey to share with others. From the beginning, the path we walked was filled with trials, but we will find ways to hold tight to the good times; the smiles, laughter, and victories which have sustaining power above all the negatives. Most of all, we had unbroken, unconditional love with our mother. We endured it all and made it through until God called her home.

We never really die. We go from this life to our eternal life—from walking and running to reaching for Jesus and being eternally healed. We are truly blessed to have such a beautiful destiny. This is the greatest promise of the Scriptures. Believe on the Lord, Jesus Christ, and receive that eternal salvation, knowing that one day we will be reunited with our loved ones. This is a blessed gift in which we can have absolute faith. Another blessing is to know that God knows we are hurting and that our rants are temporal. He understands our flesh better than we do. He never leaves our side during our grief. It may feel like He does at times, but God is faithful to those who love Him. He says He will never leave us nor forsake us, and through all of our pain and sorrow, deep down we know this is true.

---

*Wherefore we labour, that whether present
or absent, we may be accepted of him.*
2 Corinthians 5:9 KJV

We often ask ourselves, does grief ever really go away? It seems grief just lies dormant. It never really goes away and those feelings, even after years have passed, can be clearly evoked by some triggering factor or just by reminiscing. The pain of grief is still there; it just goes to sleep. That is why the quest for tranquil peace is so important ... there is peace with acceptance of loss and it helps us when those painful moments resurrect. It's a good reminder that we are not of this world, and there is a greater world beyond this one where no pain exists.

It takes a lot of courage and strength to live through grief and feel it is okay to live again, to breathe again and to laugh again. This book was started in the midst of heavy grief. It has been over two years now, and grief can still come upon us with the biting grip of a dog holding onto a bone ... but we are in a better place. The light is visible and complete peace is up ahead.

It is a great place to be, moving forward daily. We know we have to keep striving for that higher plane of life and we will! What a wonderful heavenly Father we serve! He walks with us through the valley of the shadow of death. He knows we need to do the work so we can heal and embrace that beautiful place of peace. We also have to learn to accept and embrace a different life so that we can flex the muscles of our faith to be stronger and more resilient in times of trouble.

God sees death differently than we do. He sees it as a time to rejoice. A soul has returned home to the best place forever. His ways are higher than our ways. Our loved ones are with Him, and they are happy. It's a challenge to rationalize this, at times, when we miss our loved ones so much. But it is the truth. This world is temporal. Our permanent home is with God.

> *And if I go and prepare a place for you,*
> *I will come back and take you to be with*
> *me that you also may be where I am.*
> John 14:3 NIV

If our hearts could speak for us, they would clearly express the depth and pain of our loss in far more vivid detail. But we can only write and speak our minds and, so, we are limited. It seems our minds are what keep our hearts balanced, so our hearts don't completely break. But in grief, our hearts and minds aren't always on equal footing. We rationalize things with our minds—we love with our hearts. It's a delicate balancing act. We are reminded of a line spoken in one of our favorite movies, *Steel Magnolias* (TriStar Pictures, 1989). The character M'Lynn, while standing by Shelby's casket trying to balance her grief, says, "That's what my mind says; I wish someone would explain it to my heart."

We have found one of the most important things is to be allowed to grieve without judgment. Some may get to acceptance of loss faster than others. For some, it may take quite some time. The grieving process should be respected and supported. We believe judging anyone's grief is wrong. It doesn't matter whether you lost a child, a spouse, a parent, a sibling, a grandparent, another family member, a friend or even a pet. Loss of any kind can be brutal to the person experiencing it. Grief seems to be as unique to each person as are DNA and fingerprints. We have to ask, "Can anyone really understand the depths of another person's grief?"

The grief club is one nobody wants to join but, when our time comes, we long to be with those who understand what we are going through. We have learned to find comfort with others and hope that, in some way, we help one another. This book is another contribution to a club that will always have members, but our goal is to graduate at the right time and still be there for others dealing with grief.

No one asks for an invitation, and no one wants to take the grief trip. But it is a part of life that all will experience. It is a journey everyone will go on at some point in time. Perhaps, the very fatigue it brings is a mechanism God has put in place to encourage us to leave the valley. The world is rapidly and constantly changing and has so many moving parts, and time does not stand still no matter what is going on in our personal lives, so we have to adapt while in the mayhem of brokenness.

Scripture talks about life being a race—the long race of a soul, one that we sometimes walk and sometimes run. *Walking* ... oh, how that word took on new meaning for Mama and for us. In her later years, our mother walked in pain, especially those last four months, but she cherished each and every step she took in her life. She was grateful for each time her feet met the floor. *Walking* will always have greater meaning for us now.

There is an additional bond that happens when you take care of a loved one. Sometimes we think as we grow older, losing a parent would be easier but, for us, that was not the case.

When we focus on the strengths Mama had, it inspires us to be more like her. We too are on a journey of a soul. We hope we will all complete this life as well as she did. It warms our hearts to know she walks in the sacred place called heaven.

We rejoice in the good news that God promises we can find good even in sad experiences ... so here we go. We will keep moving and keep breathing and consistently renew our minds, knowing something far more beautiful and amazing will come forth from all this pain. Each of us has our individual journey as we continue to seek and grow into a greater and more powerful faith and trust in God.

There are many things in this life we may never understand, but we choose to continue to strive to walk in God's wisdom. What becomes significant and real is the spiritual connection God puts in place. From the umbilical cord to the invisible tether to our hearts, even though her silver cord was loosed, we are forever connected to our mother's soul ... until we meet again. So to you, Mama, on every Thanksgiving Day and Christmas Day and all our days without you: through the gates of heaven our connection remains intact, preserved in love and devotion.

Looking unto Jesus the author and finisher of our faith; who for the joy that was set before him endured the cross, despising the shame, and is set down at the right hand of the throne of God.
Hebrews 12:2 KJV

Therefore being justified by faith, we have peace with God through our Lord Jesus Christ; by whom also we have access by faith into this grace wherein we stand, and rejoice in hope of the glory of God.
Romans 5:1–2 KJV

Please remember ...

Each life is indeed a treasure chest God has placed here. Each one is significant, and each one has value. Everyone has their own set of fingerprints unique only to them, and each one has a purpose only they can fulfill. All too often our treasure chest is never opened, and so many of us do not fulfill all the wonderful purposes God has placed within us. We get too caught up in the busyness of life, rarely tapping into our own genius within. Perhaps our programming may be skewed, or we lack wisdom and understanding. At times we make decisions that do not take us down the right path God has planned for us. As for our mother, while she may not have utilized *all* the treasure within her, she definitely fulfilled many of her purposes. She was a devoted wife, even in times of trouble. She was the best mother she could have been and, even with major trials and adversity, she held onto those to whom she gave birth. She fulfilled her passion and purpose for serving others. She put her talent, efforts, and skills in everything she did.

Her love for our Lord was evident, and she lived by faith, even in bleak times. Looking back now, we see how powerful her faith was. None of us realized how much she lived by that faith until we began reflecting on her life and everything we all went through together, especially in those early years. Without her faith in the Lord to bring us through, we never would have made it.

*To you, we believe Mama would say:
"Find joy in life! Remember, even in bad times,
hold on to all the good memories and find the good things
in your life to focus on to keep you moving forward.
Look to God for the power to overcome obstacles and keep
walking. Know that with God, baby steps can turn into a
marathon, and God is patient. Life here on earth is short,
but know that heaven awaits all of us for our eternal life.
Miss those who go home before you,
but let them go.*

---

*Be happy! Know that they are in the most beautiful
place." For God, who commanded the light to shine out
of darkness, hath shined in our hearts, to give the light
of the knowledge of the glory of God in the face of Jesus
Christ. But we have this treasure in earthen vessels, that
the excellency of the power may be of God, and not of us.*
2 Corinthians 4:6–7 KJV

CHAPTER 13

Reflections

Patient's Goals: ~~Walk~~ with Jesus ✓
Metas del Paciente: RUN

Written on the whiteboard in Mama's comfort care room, her grandson, Brandon, wrote that her goal now was to walk with Jesus, but when he heard about her energy and strength as she left us, he crossed out walk and wrote run, and then he check-marked that her goal was complete.

We had forgotten about the whiteboard message until we found a picture of it. We thought wow … isn't that really every Christian's goal? And in some ways aren't we all patients here on this earth, often in need of care and healing? We need nurturing in the Word on a consistent basis, and we should constantly care for ourselves physically, emotionally, mentally and spiritually. Each day we get a little closer to that ultimate patient goal as we run the race as best we know how. Such is the cycle and seasons of life. But while we are here, we are to live. No matter our trials and tribulations or our triumphs and victories, all which encompass the wholeness of the big picture; this life is temporary. It is but a vapor, here for a short while then over, but eternity is forever.

Even if we fall short at times, we have a beautiful Savior, Jesus Christ, always willing to forgive us when we repent. Such is the glory and majesty of a loving God to provide us with a system of renewal and cleansing. Through all the sadness, we are embracing all the little jewels of lessons and wisdom springing forth every day. God continues to send us many wonderful messages through Mama. Her passing has taught us so much more about the seasons of life, death, grief and faith than we ever knew before.

The shadow of our loss will always surround us, but we know Mama is alive and well in paradise, and given the choice, she would not choose to come back. This helps us in our healing and restoration. Yet there are still times, and there probably always will be times, when our minds revisit those last four months and those final days in Room 6009 where Mama would complete her journey on this earth. Perhaps we go there because we need to still feel that pain in order to keep the healing process moving forward. Perhaps we go there because those were the final months and the final precious moments we had with her. Indeed, her exit was miraculous and comforting and worth revisiting over and over again. Healing from grief is an arduous process, but we will survive. As we move forward, we are assured that the light beyond the valley will continue to guide us. The light will illuminate our memories of Mama so we can greet them with smiles on our faces and peace in our hearts.

Thinking back through the years, we are eternally grateful that Mama introduced us to Jesus Christ. It is the gift that keeps on giving us breath. Living a life of Christ wasn't fully established in our home during much of our childhood because we were more focused on survival. We endured such a mixture of inconsistent seasons in those years because we were never able to set down solid roots as a family. Now we see how this microcosm of faith, unknowingly at that time, carried us through the rough waters, just as Christ promised. That perfect seed Mama planted so many years ago, among all the weeds and thorns of our childhood, survived and grew into the living vine that continues to grow around us today. And whether we are in challenging times or good times, it will always grow mightily.

And Jesus said unto them, I am the bread of life: he that cometh to me shall never hunger, and he that believeth on me shall never thirst.
John 6:35 KJV

Abide in me, and I in you. As the branch cannot bear fruit of itself, except it abide in the vine; no more can ye, except ye abide in me. I am the vine, ye are the branches; he that abideth in me, and I in him, the same bringeth forth much fruit; for without me ye can do nothing.
John 15:4-5 KJV

As cliché as it may sound, life is very much like a puzzle. You know how we all like to find the corners and outer parts first? Why do we do that? Because it makes it easier to fill in the rest. We also look for pieces with matching colors.

Why? Because it makes it easier to put it together. But many times, it takes hours or even days to finish that puzzle and sometimes it's never finished. So we make the choice: Are we going to break it back down and put it away in the box and give it away ... or will we finish it and frame it?

We sometimes treat our lives like a puzzle. If a piece is missing, we see that puzzle as no longer having any value. Our family sees it differently now. We are given pieces to the puzzle in our lives. Some are easy to fit, but others—especially the inner pieces of our minds, thoughts, hearts, emotions, and souls—are like the pieces that have those hard colors to match up or edges that just don't fit right. We may be tempted to force-fit a piece, but that's a mistake. We have to find the perfect fit, the perfect puzzle piece. The perfection of our Lord and Savior is exclusive. He is the *only* perfect being and will always be the only perfect person. But with Him by our side, as we put our eyes and trust on Him, the pieces begin to fit together, and we learn to deal with the hard things in life by faith in Jesus.

Life is about creating this puzzle every day. There are pieces that never seem to fit. Pieces will be lost; pieces will curl up or maybe get wet. But instead of looking at the puzzle as useless because a piece is missing, we now look at it as if God has lifted that piece up, as He will throughout our lives, showing us how to work the puzzle. The piece of our puzzle missing at this time is our sweet mother that will now live forever in our hearts making it a perfect fit. Because she gave us life, she created a puzzle for us to finish to bring glory to God's name and to encourage the hearts of others whose missing pieces of their puzzle have gone to be with Him. And that beautiful piece of color and shape that made our lives whole here on earth is now rejoicing in heaven.

We hope these God-given words on paper help you on your journey through the seasons of life and your trust in God will grow more deeply to bring the whole picture together, in the end, bringing forth a new beginning.

For thou art my lamp, O LORD: and the
LORD will lighten my darkness
2 Samuel 22-29 KJV

Mama found her peace with leaving this life, as much as she loved it and loved us. She had run her race here and crossed the finish line into the arms of Jesus. We are sure that when they came face-to-face, He said, "Well done, my good and faithful servant." She finished well.

The gift we witnessed will forever be etched in our hearts. It is a reminder of how her faith and courage flowed through every season of her life. She left this world doing what was impossible with her broken earthly vessel. With legs that shouldn't be able to move, she moved with great strength. With eyes that couldn't see, she had vision. And with an arm that could barely move, she pulled away with great power, reached up and took the hand of whoever was there to show her the way to her eternal home.

Mama was at perfect peace with … Letting Go.

So here's to you, Mama …
We love you, and we promise one day we will be able to
fulfill your last request to "Miss you … but let you go!"
Until we meet again …
Your silver cord now loosed … Run free with Jesus!

*Or ever the silver cord be loosed,
or the golden bowl be broken, or the pitcher be broken
at the fountain, or the wheel broken at the cistern.
Then shall the dust return to the earth as it was;
and the spirit shall return to God who gave it.*
Ecclesiastes 12:6-7 KJV

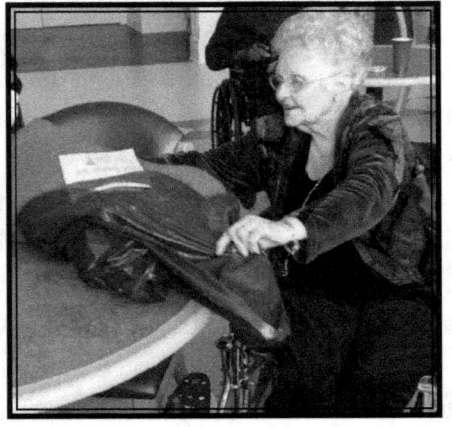

Our precious Proverbs 31 mother on February 21, 2013 receiving the beautiful red, handmade afghan the patients made for her!

Her children arise and call her blessed ...
Proverbs 28:31 NIV

*But thanks be to God, which giveth us
the victory through our Lord Jesus Christ.
Therefore, my beloved brethren, be steadfast,
unmovable, always abounding in the work
of the Lord, forasmuch as ye know that your
labour is not in vain in the Lord.*
1 Corinthians 15:57–58 KJV

*Therefore being justified by faith, we have peace
with God through our Lord Jesus Christ; by whom
also we have access by faith into this grace wherein
we stand, and rejoice in hope of the glory of God.*
Romans 5:1–2 KJV

CHAPTER 14

Signs of Wonder

As we said our final goodbyes and kissed Mama one last time, Joyce leaned into her and said, "Mama, I'm going to pray and ask God to reveal you to us through rainbows, butterflies, hearts, and beautiful clouds. We'll be looking for you, Mama, through signs of wonder."

My sweet friend Deborah took this photo. It was here I was telling Mama we would be looking for her through rainbows, butterflies, hearts, and beautiful clouds. I then gave her a final earthly kiss on her forehead.

After Mama's celebration of life service and burial, we all went back to Joyce's house, took a deep breath, and later decided to go back to the cemetery. Dealing with an overwhelming mixture of emotions and feeling the weight of extreme fatigue, we all knew we would not be able to go to sleep that night without visiting Mama.

As we stood at Mama's resting place, there was a delicate breeze twirling around us. It was about 7:15 p.m., yet the sun shone brilliantly. We were taken aback when suddenly a very soft, gentle rain began to fall upon us. Scott, one of Mama's sons-in-law, with tears in his eyes exclaimed, "Oh my gosh, look over there." We all turned and looked toward the sky, and there it was! The most beautiful, magnificent rainbow was forming. Precious to behold was this brilliant prism of light and colors that quickly became a double rainbow! We were in awe and felt Mama all around us!

Mama had written in her last wishes that her grandchildren were her sunshine and her great-grandchildren were her rainbows, and here we stood, witnessing the entire sky filled with the sun shining on one side and this amazing rainbow on the other, with this soft, swirling breeze flowing around us and caressing our faces. It was truly incredible!

Then the whole experience came full circle. As we continued looking at the rainbow, our eyes caught a glimpse of the American flag gracing the foreground of this God-made landscape of rainbows and sunshine. Even with our hearts heavy-laden with grief and our minds still absorbing this season of life we were facing, we felt deep gratitude for this precious gift. How complete a tribute to our mother, a servant to veterans and so many others, to see the rainbow flanked with the American flag as the sun shone brightly behind us. Later, many who knew her sent us pictures of the rainbow, as they saw it too and thought of Mama.

Exquisite artwork designed by the hand of Divine Providence.

While letting her go would take some time, this experience would give us strength in the coming months. The gentle breeze, the radiant sun, the colorful rainbow, the American flag and wonderful friends thinking of us and remembering Mama all came together so perfectly.

In our family, we celebrate everything, and we especially loved celebrating birthdays. As there were so many birthdays, we began to group the adult ones. All August birthdays were celebrated at one time. In August 2012, as we gathered to celebrate the birthdays of four family members and a friend, Mama surprised us when she came in with three gift boxes for her daughters. She told us she had bought them to give to us at Christmas but decided it was best to give them now.

We asked, "What? Shouldn't we wait till Christmas?"

Mama replied, "No, I want you to open them today."

When we opened our gifts, we each found a precious music box in silver and gold shaped like a big candy Kisses with a ribbon on top that said "Kisses for my daughter." The music box plays, "You Are So Beautiful to Me." On each one was attached a heart with our name engraved on it. Our hearts fell a little as we wondered if Mama had a sense of foreboding, and those Kisses for my daughter music boxes took on a whole new meaning when our unexpected future unfolded. Even the gift she gave our brother, a frame with a picture of his dog of nineteen years whom he had just previously lost, had a little heart on the frame.

Kisses for my daughters

After Mama had gone to be with Jesus, those engraved hearts took on new meaning as hearts became very significant to us. We had no idea how we would be "hearted" in the days to come! The rainbow in the cemetery was just the beginning. With our hearts and minds open to other signs, we began to see many. We believe that when you are fully open to signs, God will gift them to you. It seems that whenever we are at our lowest point, we see a sign of wonder. To this day, we continue to see butterflies, hearts, and rainbows in ways we never imagined.

Joyce had a family beach vacation planned in May. After Mama passed, it was difficult for her to think about a vacation, but her family felt she needed to go. Driving to the beach with Bradley and Megan, she hoped this trip would be a great one for them. Attending church on Sunday, her grief became overwhelming, so she sat in the car and talked to God and Mama alone. Later at Brandon and Hannah's apartment, her son Bradley set out to walk their little dog Izzie, and Joyce tagged along. Tears still welling up inside her, Joyce just really wanted to go back home. As they walked Izzie, Joyce looked up over the apartments and, to her amazement there was the most beautiful heart that had formed in a cloud. How good God is to give His children comfort. His beautiful God hugs are always there. It was beautiful, and we've always felt God allowed Mama in on this too. Bradley looked up at the heart in the clouds with a big smile and stated, "As I've always said … she rocks!"

A beautiful, peaceful heart appeared at just the right time in the last place she said she wanted to go.

Another sign of wonder showed up one bright morning when Debbie took Taylor, Mama's great-granddaughter, to Waffle House. The cook was well-known for making waffles into characters children loved. But on this day when he saw Taylor, he felt compelled to create a special waffle! When the plate was placed in front of her, Taylor became wide-eyed, and her jaw dropped. As she and Debbie gazed down at the plate, tears of joy filled their eyes because upon that plate was a waffle made into a butterfly! Debbie shared with the waitress about Mama and butterflies. The waitress called the cook over, and he said, "I have never made a butterfly waffle before, but something told me to make the little girl I saw at the table a butterfly waffle!" The waitress shared she had lost her mother two years earlier, and many hearts were touched that day at Waffle House.

Taylor's Butterfly Waffle

Hayden, Mama's great grandson, had his own "hearted" moment with a Funyon! His mother, Rebecca, always tells her children their Maw Maw is watching over them from heaven, and she will send them signs to let them know she is thinking of them. On this special moment of being "hearted," Hayden looked at the Funyon heart with wide eyes and a smile as he said, "My Maw Maw is thinking about me!"

Hayden's Funyon heart

During one of those low moments on January 4, 2014, Bonnie was "hearted" too. Just when she needed a sign, she noticed a heart-shaped object on her window. Amazed, she went outside to see exactly what it was. A piece of honeycomb had blown toward the window and stuck to it in the shape of a heart. Where the honeycomb came from is a mystery, but its sweetness came at the perfect time.

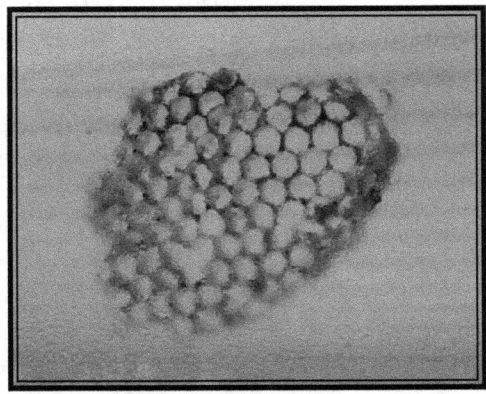

Being "hearted" became a joyous occasion!

The beauty of solar lights is how the energy from the sun fills them with energy giving them angelic light in the evening. One night around dusk, Debbie visited Mama's resting place. She was really missing Mama. As the dusk slid into darkness, she sat in her car talking to Mama, feeling the sting of grief, and then she noticed that none of Mama's solar lights were working. Disappointed, she felt her pain grow. Then suddenly, one light at a time came on until all four were bright white lights! The perfect precision of timing is what made this event so stunningly beautiful and divine. And yes, we all believe this was a sign ... a beautiful sign of wonder!

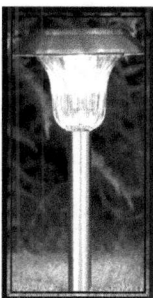

Solar lights illuminate Mama's resting place

In writing this book, we reached back into the past lives of both of our parents. We wanted to know more about our father as a young boy. In doing research, Joyce found the address of the house where our father lived with his parents and little sister Zivian. Joyce and Bonnie decided one day to go and find the house Daddy had lived in as a young boy. This was the house where pneumonia took the life of his younger sister when she was just three years old ... the house where she left to go bloom in heaven.

When we arrived at the house, we spoke with a young man who was cutting some tree branches in the front yard. We asked him if he lived there and he said no—that the house was now owned by a church and was a recovery home for women with addictions! He introduced us to the director of the recovery program, and we explained why we were there, and we asked if we could go inside.

It was such an amazing feeling to walk through this house and know the history of our father's life there. The director told us much of the house was the same as it had always been. She explained to us that the house had first been used for men who were recovering from addictions, but now the men went to another house, and this one was for women. It was a wonderful feeling to know how fitting it was that Daddy's childhood home had become a place to help others overcome the same addictions he had battled.

We saw many more signs through rainbows, butterflies, hearts and clouds that filled our souls and brought smiles to our faces. We encourage you to look for signs of wonder from your loved ones. God understands our broken hearts. He understands the world around us more than we ever will! While we are limited in the natural, He is masterful in the supernatural.

> *Trust in the Lord with all thine heart; and lean not unto thine own understanding. In all thy ways acknowledge him, and he shall direct thy paths.*
> Proverbs 3:5–6 KJV

The greatest gift given to us is Jesus—that upon his resurrection, He paved the way for our race to end here on earth and continue in heaven and that, upon repentance of sins, we are forgiven. Yes, Jesus awaits us with open arms when our race upon this earth is complete. He conquered death on the cross and the grave through His resurrection. He is the one who makes the journey of a soul a journey, in the end, of healing.

It was one of those monumentally defining moments, as we witnessed Mama's physical body prepare for her soul to leave, when the things of this earthly existence that once heralded importance, became astronomically insignificant. It was in those moments we realized how precious life and death are. Yes, even death is precious, as it is as much a part of life as life itself ... it's the letting go that is the hardest part, but we must. It is through the death of the flesh body that our soul is released, and we complete our journey to eternal life to live in another time and space, forever healed and made whole. We know in our hearts that our mother's journey came full circle exactly as God promises.

If you feel the Lord tugging on your heart, we encourage you to pause now and pray. If you want Jesus to come into your life, simply pray this prayer and turn your life over to Him.

THE PRAYER OF SALVATION

Dear God,

I know I am a sinner, and I need your forgiveness. I believe your son Jesus died on the cross and paid the penalty for my sins. I am willing right now to turn away from my sin and accept Jesus Christ as my Savior and Lord. I give my life to you and ask that you send the Holy Spirit into my life. I want to know you more and become the person you want me to be. Thank you, Father, for sending Jesus and for loving me.

In Jesus name, I pray ... Amen

Therefore he is able to save completely those who come to God through him, because he always lives to intercede for them.
Hebrews 7:25, NIV

In him you also trusted, after you heard the word of truth, the gospel of your salvation; in whom also, having believed, you were sealed with the Holy Spirit of promise.
Ephesians 1:13 NKJV

CHAPTER 15

Lasting Wishes and Messages

Our Mother impacted many lives, and many lives impacted hers. In this final section of the book, we want to share a few remembrances.

The Serenity Garden Memorial Dedication Celebrating the Life and Volunteer Work of Margaret Glenn

A memorial dedication was held August 22, 2013, in the newly created Serenity Garden at the William Jennings Bryan Dorn VA Medical Center. A beautiful table with benches was placed in the garden in Mama's memory for her fifty-one years of volunteer work and her devoted heart to the veterans. This dedication was sponsored by the SC AMVETS Auxiliary and the William Jennings Bryan Dorn VA Hospital. In attendance were dignitaries from the State AMVETS Auxiliary, the Veterans of Foreign Wars and the Veterans Hospital, as well as Pastor Terry Cagle from Greenlawn Baptist Church, where

Mama was baptized as a young lady and served many years as a member. Many family and friends were also in attendance. It was a beautiful, yet bittersweet day. Our hearts were filled to the brim with joy and gratitude for this generous dedication and being surrounded by so many people and friends who thought she was deserving of this special recognition. Yet our hearts were also filled with great sadness as we so very much missed our mama! It was beautiful and yet heartbreaking to be in a place that meant so much to her knowing her season for doing so much good work here was over.

We will forever be grateful for all involved, including the AMVETS, NEC, VA Hospital and VFW, for making this dedication possible. There was even a sweet segment of news coverage that aired on the local news. We are so thankful for all the friendships our mother made with everyone. We are thankful to them for being a light in her life.

Dedication ceremony August 22, 2013 51 years of volunteer service

A FINAL DONATION

On April 24, 2013, Mama made a donation to the Paralyzed Veterans of America organization. She was adamant that it be mailed that day and it was taken to the post office. On or about May 23rd, she received a letter thanking her for her donation. It also stated, "I have also placed the Memorial Day card you signed on the meal tray of a paralyzed veteran in remembrance of Memorial Day. Your message sends a message that rings loud and clear—you have proved you will never forget our soldiers." While we realize this was a form letter, it was still so reminiscent of the love Mama had for our veterans who serve and have served our country. It just seemed so fitting to receive this a couple of weeks after she passed. We believe Mama filled the void of losing our father, and in remembrance of his life, dedicated her service to the veterans with a heart full of love and patriotism. A perfect example of how God works through our circumstances to bring about good to fulfill His purpose.

Let your light so shine before men, that they may see your good works, and glorify your Father which is in heaven.
Matthew 5:16 KJV

LEXINGTON LIFE MAGAZINE

Lexington Life Magazine wanted to include an article about Mama in the "Servant's Heart" section of their magazine. There are so many wonderful volunteers who will never be recognized as they should be, except by God. They volunteer, not for accolades and recognition, but because they love it. But it certainly is a beautiful moment when these ordinary extraordinary women and men get a little light shone on them in hopes of encouraging others to experience volunteerism.

Quietly and subtly, Mama was a woman of influence. Not because of a career, money or political status, but because she daily influenced others through her heart and love for people.

I will love thee, O Lord, my strength. The Lord is my rock, and my fortress, and my deliverer; my God, my strength, in whom I will trust; my buckler, and the horn of my salvation, and my high tower.
Psalm 18:1–2 KJV

LASTING 'FRIEND PRINTS'

Mama's devoted hairdresser, Janie Jeffcoat, was always there for her, no matter where Mama needed Janie to fix her hair—whether it was in the hospital, in her home, or the rehab facility, Janie became the hair rescue lady that never let her down. Janie later told us that Mama was a huge source of encouragement for her and that she would miss that support system.

Diane Rainey, recreational assistant at the VA Hospital, told us that on some mornings when it was tough to get going, she would think of Mama and how she pushed through pain or whatever she had to and kept moving and that would encourage her to do the same.

Mama never knew this. It is hearing words like these that remind us how our example, a smile or a simple hello or word of encouragement to someone we know or don't know may be just what that person needed for the day. We never know how much even the smallest gesture, kind deed or act of compassion, can impact someone's life.

AN ANGEL ON EARTH

We have already mentioned Mama's nurse in the ICU, Shanika, who was relentless in trying to help Mama. She stood by Mama and us like a true guardian angel, even stating how troubled she was that they could not find the source of Mama's illness. We will always remember Shanika and her dedication to Mama and our family.

We received this beautiful note from Shanika:

> I just wanted to say thank you so much for sharing the awesome experience of your mother's home going with me. It was truly a beautiful and moving event. I literally got goosebumps all over as I was reading about it. God is so good to us and you all were blessed to be able to encounter that experience in her final moments. I also want to thank you so much for the gifts! I love the angel, candle and the perfume. You all have been so sweet to me! I don't feel that I deserve all of this attention for doing my passion because it is second nature to me.

However, it does warm my heart to know that someone is so appreciative. I thank you for the blessing you and your family have been, and I thank you for the lessons that I have learned by caring for your mother and your family ... both spiritually and clinically. You all will always remain in my thoughts and prayers.

The hospital gave its first Guardian Angel Award right after Mama passed, and we were so excited to hear that Shanika was the first recipient of this prestigious award. She will forever live in our hearts as our special guardian angel.

"Our Mother's light never grows dim in our hearts."

Excerpt from our Mother's final written words to us ...

*I want my children to know they were my reason for living and thank them from the bottom of my heart for all the joy they brought in my life.
I want to thank you for my beautiful grandchildren, my sunshine! They made every day shine for me. Love them a lot for me.
I am so proud of all of you. We had a lot of obstacles during our lifetime but with our faith and love for*

each other, we made it through— but when I stop and think, there were a lot more blessings than obstacles! I want my children to know I love the Lord with all my Heart and Soul and I am okay!! Also, even though your Dad got his life so mixed up, I still loved him so very much! We had some happy times together and those are the memories I kept. He came into my life when I was seventeen years old. I waited for him during World War II. We were married two years after he came home. You might say he was always "the one" for me and I knew this. You are his children and I know deep down in his heart he loved all of you. (We really loved each other, always remember this.) Always remember and love the Lord and keep your Faith. Let Him guide you all through your life! BE HAPPY! Mom

To my grandchildren and great-grandchildren, what a blessing! What more could a person ask for? I wish I could express how much all of you meant to me and I thank the good Lord for allowing me to stay here and enjoy every minute. Value your life, live with faith, and don't forget to love! Kiss my little Hayden and Taylor. Tell them they were my rainbows! Give my love to Jason, Brittany, Brandon, Bradley. Always remember you were my sunshine! Maw Maw.

Wherefore seeing we also are compassed about with so great a cloud of witnesses, let us lay aside every weight, and the sin which doth so easily beset us, and let us run with patience the race that is set before us, Looking unto Jesus the author and finisher of our faith; who for the joy that was set before him endured the cross, despising the shame, and is set down at the right hand of the throne of God.
Hebrews 12:1-2 KJV

Seasons of Life from the book of Ecclesiastes

To everything there is a season, and a time to every purpose under the heaven: A time to be born, and a time to die; a time to plant, and a time to pluck up that which is planted; A time to kill, and a time to heal; a time to break down, and a time to build up; A time to weep, and a time to laugh; a time to mourn, and a time to dance; A time to cast away stones, and a time to gather stones together; a time to embrace, and a time to refrain from embracing; A time to get, and a time to lose; a time to keep, and a time to cast away; A time to rend, and a time to sew; a time to keep silence, And a time to speak; A time to love, and a time to hate; a time of war, And a time of peace.
Ecclesiastes 3:1–8 KJV

ABOUT THE AUTHORS

 **Joyce Glenn Wagster** is first a daughter of the King in love with Christ and His Word, a wife, and a mother. She's a southern girl true at heart and loves family, sweet tea, and cupcakes. She began her volunteer work and found her love for singing at the age of four when her mother stood her in front of a microphone to sing for the patients at a local Veterans Hospital. The deep grief experienced through her mother's passing led her and her sister, Bonnie, to write the book, *Letting Go*. Through her ministry, as an inspirational speaker, Joyce shares her testimony about the challenges through her childhood in a family dealing with, PTSD, alcoholism and addictions. Today she graciously shares about her mother's passing and her personal journey through grief; holding on to faith and finding peace through letting go. Joyce is also a singer and author of a children's book, "Take It To The Max, Like Max!" Joyce resides in Springdale, South Carolina with her husband, Tony. They are blessed with incredible children. Brandon, their oldest son, and his wife Hannah, and their youngest son, Bradley. A special young lady, Megan is also like a daughter. Joyce and Tony have two fur babies, Buddy and Cocoa and a grand dog, Luna. For more information about Joyce's Ministry or scheduling her for an event, please visit www.joyceglennwagster.com

**Bonnie Jennings** enjoyed many years of volunteer work alongside her mother. Her mother's passing had a profound effect on her, and she entered a season of grief with pain beyond anything she could have ever imagined. One coping mechanism was writing a letter to her mother every morning and every night that first year. Simultaneously, trying to cope with her grief led her on a journey to write *Letting Go* with her sister, Joyce, in hopes of helping others in similar circumstances. She is currently co-writing a second book, *The Silver Tree*, a true life story, with her husband, Larry. She is an avid reader of the Bible. She enjoys working in ministry with her sister, Joyce. She resides in Forest Acres, South Carolina with her husband.

To learn more or to book Joyce to speak and sing at your church, women's conference, organization, or special event, please visit our website and join us on Facebook at:

www.joyceglennwagster.com
www.joycewagster@gmail.com
Facebook/Joyce Glenn Wagster
Facebook/Letting go "life before and beyond grief"

Our Mother left us beautiful messages and her final wishes in a little book that was to be opened upon her passing. This booklet has been recreated as an intimate personal guide for others to leave their lasting wishes and messages to their loved ones as well as family information and more. Make that difficult season easier by having this precious keepsake booklet ready for your family. To order e-mail OrderLettingGo@gmail.com or visit online @ www.joyceglennwagter.com

For more information on these organizations please visit their website at:

www.sepsis.org
www.amvets.org
www.ptsdusa.org

National Domestic Violence Hotline: 1-800-799-7233
Substance and Mental Abuse Hotline: 1-800-662-4357

Within the pages of this book, you will read truths about our family's journey with addictions, substance abuse, and violence. We so not endorse any of these social issues nor recommend anyone to remain with someone bringing harm through abuse and addiction. We recommend you seek wise counsel if you are in this situation.

Note from the Publisher

Are you a first time author?

Not sure how to proceed to get your book published?
Want to keep all your rights and all your royalties?
Want it to look as good as a Top 10 publisher?
Need help with editing, layout, cover design?
Want it out there selling in 90 days or less?

Visit our website for some exciting new options!

www.chalfant-eckert-publishing.com

www.ingramcontent.com/pod-product-compliance
Lightning Source LLC
LaVergne TN
LVHW051549070426
835507LV00021B/2491